CW00547984

DEALING WITH LUST AND GREED

ACCORDING TO ISLAM

Sheikh 'Abd al-Hamid Kishk

© Dar Al Taqwa Ltd. 1995

ISBN 1 870582 40 3

All rights reserved. No part of this publication may be reproduced, stored in a retrieval system, or transmitted, in any form or by any means, electronic, mechanical, photocopying, recording or otherwise, without the prior permission of the publishers.

Translation: *Aisha Bewley*

Editors: *Abdalhaqq Bewley and Muhammad 'Isa Waley*

Production: *Bookwork, Slough.*

Published by:
Dar Al Taqwa Ltd.
7A Melcombe Street
Baker Street
London NW1 6AE

Printed in Great Britain by:

Deluxe Printers
245A Acton Lane
Park Royal
London NW10 7NR

Tel: 0181-965-1771

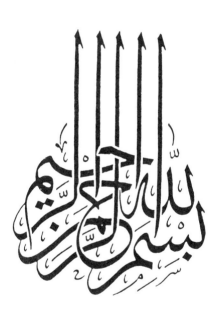

Table of Contents

Preface

O Allah, bless our master, our beloved Prophet, Muhammad
ibn 'Abdullah, the balm and cure of our hearts, the healing and
well-being of our bodies, and the light and illumination of our
eyes, the noblest of creatures and the Master of the Messengers
who was sent as a mercy to all human beings to bring them out of
the constriction of this world into the expansion of the Next World
and out of the darkness of their lower appetites into the light of
guidance and the Clear Truth.

I have written this book in response to the numerous questions
posed to me by young Muslims in the East and the West concerning the struggle taking place between their lower selves, which
pursue their desires and appetites, and their souls, which yearn for
purity and perfection and to follow the Path of Truth. Their struggle is between human nature, which is predisposed to the love of
the lower appetites, and the Islamic Way which they freely choose
and desire to follow as their *deen*.

How should these young people face that struggle which is in
danger of taking them so far from the Path of Allah? How can they
gain the upper hand in it? How can they free themselves from the
shackles of the lower self and its appetites, and master them and
not be mastered by them? What should they do when their selves
which command to evil urge them to commit fornication? What
offence is more conducive to perdition and destruction? The sexual appetite is a natural instinct which is most beneficial if kept
within the proper limits. However, if it is allowed free rein it
brings about destruction and ruin and even its awakening is a
cause for alarm. What should they do when love of wealth overcomes them and induces them to steal? Even if they can avoid the

punishment of the law, they still have enough light to make them fear Divine Retribution.

To these and others I dedicate this book inspired by Allah's words:

> *"Believing men and women are protectors and friends of one another. They enjoin the right and forbid the wrong."* (9:71)

I offer it out of my deep faith in the perfect aptitude of Islam to identify the disease and prescribe its treatment. Islam is a practical path which has unfurled the banners of truth and justice over all the earth and poured forth oceans of pure water to cleanse the earth of all its filth, dirt, and impurities. For the Muslims it ensures might, nobility, and tranquillity and everything for which man searches on the face of the earth. They are embraced by the words of Allah Almighty:

> *"All those who follow My guidance will not go astray nor will they be miserable. But anyone who turns away from My reminder, his life will be a dark and narrow one and on the Day of Rising We will gather him blind."*
> (20:123-124)

I dedicate this book to all who are subject to their lower appetites which alienate them from the path of good, love and beauty, but are determined to struggle against those appetites and desires with truthfulness, determination and sincerity; to struggle so that Allah can free their hearts from the turmoil of that struggle and grant them the coolness of true certainty; to struggle to bring about a society which desires to follow the path of light towards true progress, justice, and civilisation; and to struggle to be free from enslavement to their lower appetites which bring inevitable destruction in their wake:

> *"You were on the very brink of a pit of the Fire and He saved you from it. In this way Allah makes His Signs clear to you, so that perhaps you will be guided."* (3:103)

2

I dedicate this book to all such people. We are living within the compass of the illuminating *ayats* of the Qur'an which were revealed to give light to our lives both in this world and the Next. The *ayats* were brought down by the Faithful Spirit to him whom Allah sent as a mercy to all the worlds so that there would be clear guidance for all who have hearts to respond and ears to hear. Therefore let us listen and awaken our hearts and hearken to the words of the Merciful and Compassionate:

"*Anyone Allah guides, he it is who is guided. Anyone He leads astray, you will not find any protector to guide him right.*" (18:17)

"*Anyone who holds fast to Allah has been guided to a straight path.*" (2:101)

"*Anyone who holds fast to Allah has been guided to a straight path.*" (24:40)

"*Anyone Allah humiliates will have none to honour him.*" (22:18)

"*O Mankind, an admonition has come to you from your Lord, and healing for what is in the breasts, and guidance and mercy for the believers. Say: 'The overflowing favour of Allah and His mercy, it is in that that they should rejoice. That is better than anything they accumulate.'*" (10:57-58)

We ask Allah that this book may have been written for His pleasure alone and that its readers may benefit from it! Knowledge is like rain which falls on people's hearts and removes their impurities, and falls on their intellects and illuminates them. Allah is Him whose help we ask. Allah is enough for us and the best of guardians.

Chapter One
The Definition of the Appetites and their Different Categories

An appetite is the desire of the lower self to obtain something which it imagines will satisfy it or give it enjoyment. People say, "This food accords with so-and-so's appetite," meaning that it is what he or she really likes. The human self accords great importance to its appetites. If the appetites are given free rein, people will continually seek more and more of what will lead them to destruction. They will be destroyed because they will go beyond the limits and leave the right path. It is therefore necessary for people to curb their appetites and hold themselves to contentment with little:

The more you give the lower self, the more it wants.
If you keep it used to little, it remains content.

This means that the lower appetites should always be kept in check by the impregnable bulwark of the intellect. They are necessary as fuel for life in this world but anyone who constantly gives in to them becomes addicted to this world and happy with it alone at the expense of the Next World. Man is both spirit and body. His spirit wants him to rise to sublime heights and to be given its own requirements in terms of the Qur'an and pure *Sunna* and various good actions such as prayer, fasting, *zakat*, maintaining ties of kinship, truthful speech, kindness, gentleness and forbearance, and keeping contracts.

The body only really has need of a small number of material things: enough to keep the back straight. If it has them, the lower self will be content and not go beyond the limits. It will command you to do right and forbid you to do wrong and be a helpmate for you both in your *deen* and this world. But if a man is distracted by the bodily world from the spiritual world, his lower self will inevitably lag behind the caravan of faith and he will become preoccupied with its demands, excesses and impetuosity. He will be like an unruly horse which wanders all over the place with nothing to restrain it, no goal to head towards and no clear path to follow. We seek refuge with Allah! That is pure wretchedness, a miserable life of complete failure.

The appetites - the gateway to the Fire

It is related that the Prophet, may Allah bless him and grant him peace, said, "The Fire is surrounded by appetites and the Garden is surrounded by difficult things."

The explanation of that statement of the Prophet can be found in another *hadith*: "Allah Almighty created the Fire, and He said to Jibril, 'Go and look at it.' He went and looked at it and said, 'By Your Might, no one will hear of it and then enter it!' Then Allah surrounded it with appetites and said, 'Now go and look it.' So he went and looked at it and said, 'By Your Might, now I fear that no one will be saved from entering it!' He created the Garden and said to Jibril, 'Go and look at it. He went and looked at it and said, 'By Your Might, no one will hear of it without entering it!' Then He surrounded it with difficult things and then said, 'Go and look at it.' He (Jibril) went and looked at it and said, 'By Your Might, I fear that now no one will enter it!'"

So anyone who forces his heart to give up the things which it desires and which his lower self yearns for but which his Lord dislikes has protected himself from the Fire and has made it mandatory for Allah to safeguard him from it. Most of the actions which Allah Almighty has commanded and encouraged are irksome for the heart and tiring for the limbs. They are things that tend to be contrary to human nature and burdensome for the lower self.

Allah knew His creation and what was in the best interests of His slaves before He created them. He knew that it is part of human nature to like what agrees with it and dislike what opposes it. The appetites leap towards the one and the lower self rejects the other. No one would leave what his lower self desires without the threat of the painful punishment which is awaiting it if it does not; and no one would put up with difficulties without the hope and promise of the endless bliss which is awaiting him if he does. People only abandon their appetites and endure difficulties on account of fear and hope. The Almighty, therefore, frightens His slaves and threatens them and He gives them hope and makes promises to them so that they may fear Him and have hope in Him.

This is how Allah describes those who understand that and fear Him:

"But as for him who feared the Station of his Lord and forbade the lower self its appetites, the Garden is his refuge." (79:40)

Allah Almighty says that when someone fears his Lord, he forbids the lower self its appetites. In other words, godfearing people flee from and avoid what Allah has forbidden. Allah describes them when he says:

"That is for those who fear My station and fear My threat." (14:14)

Appetite constitutes a strong psychological force which is woven together with the personality and the bodily needs. Some of it is necessary for the perpetuation of human existence on the face of the earth. But excess of it is the source of all conflict from the beginning of creation until now. Conflict within the family is the result of the desire for food, dress, adornment and the various other desires of the lower self. Conflict between nations is the result of the desire for wealth in various forms and the desire for power and for exploitation of the goods of other people.

Allah's Messengers and Messages came one after the other only in order to remedy these appetites which are created in man as a test and a trial for him. They show us how to apply our wills to keep our bodily needs within certain beneficial limits and enable us to use our intellects to reflect on the vast dominions of the heavens and the earth; and that in turn enables us to affirm the greatness of our Creator so that we may humble ourselves before Him as sincere believers. This is our true role in existence. We are not merely animals striving to satisfy our instincts, devoting all our energy, possessions and life to that alone.

Allah created man to replenish existence by his intellect and effort, to disseminate security, justice and prosperity, and to combat ignorance, injustice and oppression. Allah created him to strive against his lower self which commands him to evil and gave him inner strength to enable him to confront the hardships and difficulties of life. That is what truly constitutes human life. A life of affluence, pleasures, and fulfilment of appetites is in reality death itself, because it means that man has gravitated to the earth and followed his lower appetites. Allah Almighty says:

> "If We had willed, We would have raised him up by them. However, he gravitated towards the earth and followed his base desires. His likeness is that of a dog: if you chase it away, it lolls out its tongue, and if you leave it be, it lolls out its tongue. That is the likeness of people who deny Our signs. Therefore tell the story, so that perhaps they will reflect." (7:176)

The clear Signs of Allah are nourishment for the spirit and intellect. They are a clear light which enters the breast and breathes life into the human self and treats its illnesses which take the form of never-ending desires. Whenever someone satisfies one of the desires of his lower self, it says to him, "Isn't there any more?" If it is given free rein, it will inevitably cast him into a bottomless pit and deeper and deeper darkness:

8

*"Or is someone who was dead and then We brought him
to life and supplied him with a light by which to walk
among the people, the same as someone in utter darkness,
unable to get out of it? In that way the things they were
doing are made to appear attractive to the rejectors."*
(6:122)

Could there be any darkness blacker for man than the prison of
his lower self which continually demands him to give it what it
wants and will not let him go when he tries to escape its clutches?
How can he escape when he has made it his leader and has become
its hostage even though it is his most hostile enemy? He has not
corralled it within the stockade of the *Shari'a,* so it has imprisoned
him within the dark dungeon of his appetites. The result is that we
find blind humanity stumbling about in the darkness of misguidance, all the time imagining that they are doing good:

*"Say: 'Shall I inform you of the greatest losers in
respect of their actions? Those whose striving in the life of
this world is misguided while they suppose that they are
doing good.' Those are the people who reject the signs of
their Lord and the meeting with Him. Their actions come
to nothing and, on the Day of Rising, We shall assign no
weight to them."* (18:103-105)

O Allah, include us among those who listen to Your words and
follow them; those who are illuminated by the light of Islam; those
who discipline their selves so that they become content and their
appetites die away. Our beloved Prophet said: "When light enters
the heart, the breast expands for it and opens up." He was asked,
"O Messenger of Allah, is there a sign by which that can be recognised?" He said, "Yes, it brings about aversion to the Abode of
Delusion and action for the Abode of Eternity and preparation for
death before it comes." When light comes the appetites die down
and the demands of the lower self cease their clamour so that it no
longer commands us to evil or asks us to do what is forbidden. We

are only concerned with hastening to good deeds and racing to take advantage of all the hours and moments which remain to us. That is because we become aware that our lives are going to end and with them the possibility of good action.

The different categories of appetites

Enumerating the great variety of appetites is a matter of some difficulty because it is connected to the entangled and interwoven desires of the lower self. It is, of course, in the Noble Qur'an that we find the most comprehensive listing of the appetites. They are placed in principal categories with numerous derivative secondary branches stemming from them. Allah Almighty is the Creator of the human self and its Master. He is Wise and Aware of every human characteristic, high and low, secret and open. He says in His Noble Book:

> "To mankind the love of worldly appetites is painted in
> glowing colours: women and children, heaped-up mounds
> of gold and silver, horses with distinctive markings, live-
> stock, and fertile farmland. All that is merely the enjoy-
> ment of the life of this world. But the best homecoming is
> into the presence of Allah." (3:14)

The fact that 'love of worldly appetites is painted in glowing colours' means that people actually approve of loving them and see nothing ugly or any fault in doing that. They almost never abandon them. It is a very strong kind of love and people in its grip rarely see its ugliness or harmfulness even though it is both ugly and harmful. So they do not want to leave it even though it is harmful for them. It is possible to love something even though you know it is evil and not good, harmful and not beneficial. You desire it in spite of that; like some people who smoke even though it causes them harm. If love of a thing is not painted in glowing colours, you always have the possibility of leaving it but if it is, it is almost impossible to give it up.

Allah has created people with a love of worldly appetites, as the *ayat* makes clear, as a sort of test for them. If someone becomes dependent on them and is happy with them, they become his constant preoccupation and distract him from striving to draw near to his Lord. His dense material nature overcomes his luminous spiritual nature. However, if people do strive for Allah as they should, not letting their worldly appetites distract them from the path of reaching their Lord, they will have the highest degrees of the Garden because they have passed the test of their Lord with distinction:

> *"We made everything on the earth adornment for it so that We could test them to see which of them is best in action."* (18:7)

In the *ayat* Allah mentions six distinct appetites whose love occupies the hearts of mankind and which distract them from their *deen*. They are the basis of all their trials in this life.

1: Love of women

Women are the goal of the sexual appetite and the focus of desirous looks and in them the lower self finds its repose. The Almighty says:

> *"Among His signs is that He created for you spouses from yourselves so that you might find repose with them. And He has placed between you affection and mercy."*
> (30:20)

Men spend most of what they earn on women and are their overseers because of their strength and their ability to protect them. If this appetite is confined within the limits prescribed by the *Shari'a* of Islam, it is a good thing and a blessing for society because it involves the establishment of the Muslim family on firm foundations of love, mercy and affection. It is no wonder that one

11

of the first commands which issued from the Almighty to Adam was:

"Adam, live, you and your wife, in the Garden." (2:34)

Allah did not say to him: "Live alone in the garden," or "Live, you and your lover, in the Garden." He said to him, "Live, you and your wife..." So Islam, the religion of Truth, calls for marriage and recommends it and urges it so that people will not be burdened with something they will not be able to bear. The sexual drive is a natural instinct which is beneficial if kept within limits but causes destruction and ruin if allowed free rein.

For this reason Islam, with its true *Shari'a*, does not allow fornication. Fornication is a descent into vice, a plunge into a foul morass. Allah Almighty has connected the sin of fornication with idolworship and murder and He has made the punishment for it to remain forever in the Fire in terrible, humiliating torment unless that is removed by sincere repentance, belief and righteous actions.

Islam guides people to purification and purity. It establishes pure morals founded on fidelity and virtue. It flows like the pure sea to cleanse the earth of its filth, dirt and every impurity.

Allah put love of women before love of children. Love of children does not contain the same excess and extravagance as love of women. There are many men who exalt the love of women over the love of their children and so neglect their upbringing and deprive them of provision. There are many wealthy and powerful men who condemn their children to a life a poverty and abasement because they love another woman more than their mother. They become obsessed with such women and their passion distracts them from every duty. This is a great danger for society as a whole.

2: Love of children

What is meant here are children in general. The Almighty says:

"Your wealth and your children are only a trial."
(64:15)

The natural basis of love of wives and love of children is one
and the same thing: preservation of the species together with the
desire for immortality. It is the reverberating echo of Shaytan's
whispered words to Adam:

*"Shall I show you the way to the Tree of Everlasting Life
and to a kingdom which will never fade away?"* (20:120)

Love for sons is stronger than love for daughters for many reasons. Among them is the fact that sons are the basis of lineage by
which uninterrupted lines of descent are continued. Sons maintain
that fame and praise among people which most men covet. The
hope of the parents is that their sons will care for them in the
weakness of old age. They have expectations of them which they
do not have of women, such as brilliance in knowledge and deed
or leadership in society. There is also the continual awareness than
when a woman grows up, she will leave her family and join another family.

When the instinctive love of children is surrounded by the
unassailable stockade of the *Shari'a* it can certainly be considered
a praiseworthy instinct because it makes a man cheerfully endure
the burdens of his family and the upbringing of his children and
this helps him perform his other tasks in life with resolve and trust
in what Allah has prepared for him in the Next World. However,
sometimes love of children exceeds these praiseworthy limits and
turns children from being a means to the attainment of the pleasure
of Allah into people's sole goal in life. When that happens people
spend their lives striving for the sake of their children alone and
pay no attention to the remembrance of Allah and obedience to
Him.

That is a great calamity since people then strive for the sake of
their children and not in order to make the word of Allah upper-
most. They expend their wealth and energy and squander their
time for the sake of their children alone and do not maintain ties of
kinship or promote the advancement of their society. They have

turned from the worship of Allah to the worship of children. When the means becomes the end the balance of life is upset and the *Shari'a* of Allah is neglected. Allah cautions us against this in the strongest terms in clear explicit *ayats*. He says:

"O you who believe! Do not allow your wealth or your children to divert you from the remembrance of Allah. If anyone does that, they are the losers." (63:10)

"O you who believe! In your wives and your children there is an enemy for you so beware of them. But if you pardon and overlook and forgive, Allah is Forgiving, Merciful." (64:14)

Could there be any worse enemy than tribulation in your *deen*? Iblis the accursed is only considered to be an implacable enemy because he waits for us on the Straight Path and diverts us from remembrance of Allah. He flows through our veins like blood and awakens in us the appetite of excessive love for children which leads us off the path of truth and distances us from the pleasure of Allah. Our children then become a barrier on our path to the Garden because we are distracted by them and make them the sole purpose of our lives. This is how our children turn into our enemies. The same applies to wives if they become our sole focus. We seek refuge with Allah!

The Almighty also says by way of warning against excessive love of children:

"It is not your wealth or your children which bring you close in nearness to Us, except in the case of those who believe and act rightly. Those will have a double recompense for what they did. They will be safe from all harm in the highest part of Paradise." (34:37)

"Your relatives and your children will not benefit you on the Day of Rising. He will distinguish between you. Allah sees everything you do." (60:3)

"Know that your wealth and your children are a trial, and that with Allah there is an enormous wage." (8:28)

14

"Say: 'If your fathers or your sons or your brothers or your wives or your tribe, or any wealth you have acquired, or any business you fear may decline, or any dwellings which please you, are dearer to you than Allah and His Messenger and performing jihad in His way, then wait until Allah brings about His command. Allah does not guide people who are wantonly deviant.'" (9:24)

"Do not admire their wealth and their children. Allah merely desires to punish them by them during the life of this world, and for their souls to depart while they are still rejectors." (9:55)

"Neither their wealth nor their children will avail them in any way against Allah. Those are the Companions of the Fire. They are in it timelessly, forever." (58:17)

"O Mankind! Be fearful of your Lord and fear a Day when no father will be able to compensate for his son, and no son able to compensate for his father, in any way. Allah's promise is true. Do not, therefore, let the life of this world delude you and do not let the Deluder delude you concerning Allah." (31:33)

Once you have read these radiant *ayats* which light our way and make our steps firm on the path of belief, you will know, my brother Muslim, that your children are an enormous trial for you and that you must not let Shaytan delude you by making you over-preoccupied with them. He does this by whispering words which are true but whose aim is false. He will assert that they are a trust for which you are responsible and that you will have a reward with Allah for all that you spend on them as well as for any hardships you endure for their sake.

These things are true but when the limit is overstepped so that your life becomes entirely devoted to them and you make them your sole focus and make them the recipients of all you own without the beggar and destitute having any share in your wealth, then know that by doing that you have left the way of Allah and turned aside from His remembrance. You will find that the statement of the Prophet: "Whoever loves something is punished by it," becomes true of you. Those very children will become the source of your misery and wretchedness. You will not receive any solace from them because you have not built your life on the solid foundation of fear of Allah. You have built it, in fact, on the brink of a crumbling cliff-edge of appetites and it will fall over taking you with it. Then you will be left with nothing but repentance and regret which will usher in a time of bitter remorse. Look at the comprehensive nature of the supplication which Ibrahim made to his Lord:

> *"And do not disgrace me on the Day they are raised up,*
> *the Day that neither wealth nor sons will be of any benefit,*
> *except to those who bring to Allah untainted hearts."*
> (26:87-89)

O Allah, prevent us from becoming preoccupied with this world through its adornment and attractiveness and pleasures! Put it in our hands but not in our hearts. You have power over everything and are the Answerer of our prayers.

3: Love of heaped-up mounds of gold and silver

By "mounds", the Arabs mean abundant wealth, and "heaped-up" is added to it by way of emphasis. The expression gives the idea of an abundance which is the cause of temptation: something which preoccupies the heart to such an extent that there is no time or room for awareness of the need to pursue the Truth and prepare for the Next World. In every nation it is always the wealthy who are the first to reject the mission of their Messengers and to be arrogant about answering their call. And even if they do respond and believe, they are the people who do least and are furthest from the guidance of the *deen*. Look at the words of the Almighty:

> *"The desert Arabs who remained behind will say to you,*
> *'Our possessions and our family kept us occupied, so ask*
> *forgiveness for us.'"* (48:11)

16

Love of property is part of human nature and is intermingled with the flesh and blood of human beings. Man's desires are limitless and cannot be counted or enumerated. Whenever anyone gains pleasure he seeks more of it. People never reach the end of their pursuit of wealth but continually want more and more to the point that their voracity sometimes leads them to forget that it is only a means and not an end in itself. They will use any method to obtain it and cease to be concerned about whether it is lawful or unlawful. Al-Bukhari and Muslim related from Ibn 'Abbas that the Prophet said, "If the son of Adam had two valleys of gold, he would still want a third. But the belly of the son of Adam will only be filled by dust. But Allah turns to the one who turns in repentance."

The temptation of wealth dazzles many people and blinds them to the rights of Allah and the rights of their community and country, often to the rights of those they deal with, sometimes even to the rights of their families, and in extreme cases to the rights they owe to themselves. Malik al-Ash'ari said that he heard the Messenger of Allah, may Allah bless him and grant him peace, say, "I only fear three things for my community: that they will acquire great wealth and then envy one another and fight one another other; that understanding of the Book will be opened to them and believers will begin to seek its inner meanings, when only Allah and those firmly rooted in knowledge who say, 'We believe in all of it,' truly know them; and that their knowledge will increase and they will waste it and not enquire further about it."

4: Love of horses with distinctive markings

These are the horses which are grazed in green pastures. They include all horses bought for trading purposes and those finely bred horses with distinctive markings which the great and rich acquire as part of their wealth and which they use to vaunt themselves over other people. Some people go to such extremes in this that it became an obsession on the edge of insanity. Nowadays cars might be said to take the place of horses.

5: Love of livestock

This constitutes the main form of wealth of desert people and that in which their affluence, livelihood and comfort resides. They boast about them and are always seeking to have more. The term includes animal wealth of every kind.

6: Love of farmland

This is, of course, the basis of all human and animal life in town and country throughout the world and there is, in fact, greater real need for it than for any of the previous categories and its benefit is greater because of the use it is put to. The more it is actually used the less it is merely a garnish for people's desires. Proper use of it seldom impedes preparation for the Next World or prevents support of the Truth. There is nothing of more universal use and greater benefit than light, air water and land. Those who are alive cannot dispense with them but people rarely pay enough attention to them or give them the consideration they deserve.

✳✶✳✶✳

It is evident that two of these six appetites are connected to women and children and that the remaining four are connected to wealth either in terms of money or of goods. That is because of the importance held by wealth in human affairs and the prominent part it plays in establishing life and furthering it and in providing the ease and luxury so dear to man. Wealth is, moreover, the basic means of realising all other human appetites.

Wealth is a blessing when it is directed towards virtue and a punishment when it is directed towards vice. It is the bulwark of the community and its succour, honour and strength when it is restricted to the way of Allah and spent in the clearly defined channels which are proper for it: *jihad* in the way of Allah; encouraging social solidarity between the Muslims; providing for relatives, orphans, the destitute, and travellers; fulfilling other people's rights and returning things held on trust to their owners; and not devouring other people's property wrongfully through usury, theft, fraud, bribery, or usurpation of their rights.

All of this was clarified by our beloved Prophet in succinct far-reaching words which show us with light, purity and integrity how wealth should circulate in a Muslim society. He said, "Wealth is verdant and sweet. It is an excellent companion for the Muslim who gives some of it to the poor, the orphan and the traveller. But if he takes it without having any right to it, he is like someone who eats and does not become full and it will be a witness against him on the Day of Rising."

He, may the blessings and peace of my Lord be on him, says almost the same thing to us in another *hadith*: "Wealth is verdant and sweet. Anyone who takes it reluctantly will be blessed in it but anyone who takes it with the uncritical approval of his lower self, namely with avarice and greed, will not be blessed in it. He is like someone who eats and does not become full."

The "reluctance" referred to here means contentment, moderation and honour: honour in respect of the means and honour in respect of the end. The "uncritical approval" referred to means avid greed and vile degenerateness. Our great teacher indicates that we should rein in the appetite for wealth by means of the halter of the *Shari'a*. His words begin with an awareness of the desire for wealth in the being of man and teach us the basic criteria governing the circulation of wealth in society and then go beyond that into the realm of acquisition and earning.

The Prophet, may Allah bless him and grant him peace, also said, "O people! Fear Allah and be moderate in what you demand. No one will die until he has obtained the entire amount of his provision even though its arrival might be delayed. Fear Allah and be moderate in what you demand. Take what is lawful and leave what is unlawful. Do not let delay in the arrival of your provision move you to take it through disobedience to Allah. What is with Allah can only be obtained by obeying Him."

Any examination of the teachings of Islam concerning the correct way of dealing with the appetites inevitably causes us to be overwhelmed by the vast generosity of the One who is All-Wise, All-Aware, and Endlessly Kind to His slaves. It fills us with certainty that our master Muhammad is indeed the Messenger of Allah to all mankind, the mentor of humanity and their greatest teacher who will bring them out of the darkness to the light.

Come with me, my brother Muslim, and let us scoop up handfuls from the stream of the Most High and All-Powerful and take a drink from that pure radiance which will bring us out of the darkness into the light; which will release us from the constriction, darkness and appetites of our lower selves into the lofty realms of the spiritual worlds; and which will allow us to behold those vast horizons which open onto the Hidden Dominions of the heavens and the earth.

We will learn the detailed steps of the Islamic method of regulating the lower appetites in three successive stages which will enable us, with Allah's permission, to achieve that exalted goal. These stages are:

1. The Islamic remedy for excessive love of women.
2. The Islamic remedy for excessive love of children.
3. The Islamic remedy for excessive love of wealth.

Chapter Two
The Remedy for Excessive Love of Women

Love of women originates in the sexual instinct which is one of the basic constituents of the human being. It is undoubtedly necessary for sexual intercourse, procreation and the populating of the world. It is the strongest of all the instincts and the most dangerous if not contained within the unassailable stockade of the *Shari'a* of Allah which protects it, keeps it in check and directs it in a healthy direction for the well-being of Muslim society.

The word instinct (*gharîza*) comes from the verb *gharaza*, meaning that it is something implanted and imbedded in man. So the roots of the sexual instinct permeate right through man. He can never be completely free of it. Then the roots turn into trunk, boughs, branches and fruit. Islam takes a wise position in relation to this tree of sexuality by watering it with the water of modesty, purity and chastity, and so training its branches and leaves that it produces fruit in a manner pleasing to Allah and His Messenger.

That is why clear limits and precise rules have been laid down on how men and women should interact and how women should be treated so that there will be no confusion in Muslim society. Most of those who end up in the Fire do so because they made light of certain evils. Those who reflect on the *ayats* of Allah will find that Allah concludes His prescription of most of His limits with His words: *"These are the limits of Allah, so do not overstep them"* (2:229), except in the case of fornication when Allah Almighty says: *"And do not go near to fornication. It is an indecent act, an evil way"* (17:32). Allah singles it out in this way because of its seriousness and its consequences.

The mere fact of approaching the limits of fornication often causes a person to fall into it because it is connected to emotions

21

and instincts that are an integral part of a man's being. He cannot repel them. The lower self commands to evil and the urges of the sexual appetite are like the tumultuous waves of a sea which cannot be held back. He is surrounded by them on every side and they carry him along until he plunges into the abyss.

If that happens man will have only himself to blame because he did not hold to the teachings of his Lord which are there to guide him to circumspection and safety. He will see that he was driven by whims and desires, misleading deceptions and corrupting company until he deviated far from the way of truth and found himself on the brink of a pit of the Fire or a crumbling cliff-edge which was about to fall taking him with it:

> "Allah desires to turn towards you, but those who pursue their base appetites desire to make you deviate completely. Allah desires to make things lighter for you. Man was created weak." (4:27-28).

This is a true statement from Him who is All-Wise, All-Aware. Man is weak because of the appetites imbedded in him. How could disdain for the limits of Allah and indulgence in falsehood possibly lead to liberty, fraternity or equality? This means that such political slogans are in reality a hidden call to awaken the lower appetites and unleash them, causing people to wallow in error and misguidance. Why should we have disdain for the limits of Allah when He has stipulated them for us to diminish the compulsion and vigour of our appetites that cause corruption and grief for us which we could well do without? Why should we want to take the path of shaytans and follow them and leave the path of the Merciful and Compassionate who knew all about our weakness before He created us? He merely wants to spare us the evils of our lower selves and our bad actions.

The fact is that the All-Merciful did not give us a completely free rein so that a man might take his appetites for his god. Rather He cautions us and warns us and makes the punishment for fornication the most severe punishment in this world and the Next so that it spells ruin to the life of any heedless, rebellious couple who commit it. There is sufficient warning to set alarm bells ringing in the ears of any couple who consider it and to awaken their consciences and show them that they are advancing towards terrors which would make children white-haired.

In explanation of the words of Allah about Hell, *"It has seven gates"*, the commentator 'Ata' said, "The worst of the gates in respect of grief, heat and torment and the one with the foulest stench is the gate of the fornicators who committed fornication knowing it to be wrong." My brother Muslim, look at the *ayats* of the Qur'an which call on us to guard our private parts:

> *"It is the believers who are successful: those who are humble in their prayer; those who turn away from prattle; those who are active in paying zakat; those who guard their private parts - except from their wives or what their right hands own, in that case not being blameworthy; but any desiring anything more than that, they are the oversteppers of the limits."* (23:1-7)

What overstepping could be worse than violating someone's honour? It is unlawful for a Muslim to harm another Muslim, his property or his honour, as the Prophet, may Allah bless him and grant him peace, said.

> *"Say to the believing men that they should lower their eyes and guard their private parts. That is purer for them. Allah is aware of what they do. Say to the believing women that they should lower their eyes and guard their private parts and not disclose their adornments, except for that which ordinarily appears, and should draw their head-coverings across their breasts. They must not disclose their adornments except to their husbands or their fathers or their husbands' fathers, or their sons or their husbands' sons or their brothers or their brothers' sons or their sisters' sons or other women or what their right hands own or their male attendants who have no sexual desire or children who still have no consciousness of*

women's private parts. Nor should they stamp their feet so that their hidden ornaments are known. Turn to Allah, o believers, every one of you, so that perhaps you will have success."

(24:30-31)

My brother Muslim, just look at these fine lines and the clear path they delineate enabling each Muslim man and woman to achieve purity and chastity. They are predominantly directed at women because it is they who are the focus of men's attraction and because the primary responsibility for shutting the openings of Shaytan which lead to sexual desire between the sexes lies in their hands. Without a doubt, this is an extremely important responsibility. Allah's instructions regarding this matter are concluded in *Surat al-Ahzab* when He is addressing the wives of the Prophet and every Muslim woman who follows them in the path of belief:

"O wives of the Prophet! If any of you commit a clear act of indecency she will get double the punishment. That is an easy matter for Allah. But each of you who is obedient to Allah and His Messenger and acts rightly will be given her wage twice over and We have prepared generous provision for her. O wives of the Prophet! You are not like other women provided you are godfearing. Do not be soft in your speech in case someone with sickness in his heart becomes desirous. Speak correct and courteous words. Remain in your houses and do not display your beauty as it was displayed formerly in the Days of Ignorance. Establish the prayer and pay the zakat. Obey Allah and His Messenger. Allah desires to remove all impurity from you, o People of the House, and to purify you completely." (33:30-33)

"O Prophet! Tell your wives and daughters and the believing women to draw their outer garments closely round themselves. That makes it more likely they will be recognised and not be harmed. Allah is Forgiving, Merciful." (33:59)

The path of safeguarding the private parts

In these clear *ayats* Allah has delineated a clearly marked path showing us how to safeguard our private parts. He has not left any loopholes. It is a firm path with a firm foundation which precludes the approach of wrongdoing from all directions. The milestones along that path are as folows:

1: Lowering the eyes

Allah Almighty instructed His Prophet to order the believers to lower their eyes and guard their private parts and to inform them that He witnesses their actions and is aware of them. "He knows the surreptitious glances and the thoughts concealed in man's breast." Lewd behaviour generally starts with the eyes and so He gave the command to lower them before mentioning safeguarding the private parts. Sexual attraction begins with a mere glance in the same way that the starting point for the majority of the people of the Fire is some minor wrong action. First comes the glance, then the thought, then the step and then the offence. This is why it is said: "Anyone who is safe from four things preserves his *deen:* glances, thoughts, words and steps." So people must guard themselves at these four gates in their defensive walls. They are a way for the enemy to enter and open breaches in order to destroy what is above them completely.

The Prophet, may Allah bless him and grant him peace, said, "O 'Ali, do not follow one glance with a second one. The first is all right but not the second." The Prophet, may Allah bless him and grant him peace, also said, "The glance is a poisoned arrow from the quiver of Iblis. If anyone restrains his glance from looking at the beauties of women, Allah will transmit to his heart the sweetness of worship until the Day of Rising." He further said, "Lower your eyes and protect your private parts." Ahmad ibn Hanbal related this in the *hadith* which starts: "Guarantee me six things from yourselves." He said as well, "Beware of sitting at the roadside." They said, "Messenger of Allah, we have to sit there." He said, "If you must do it, then give the roadway its due." They

25

said, "What is its due?" He said, "To lower the eyes, refrain from causing injury, and return greetings."

The glance is at the root of most of the calamities which beset man. The glance engenders the thought which then becomes strong and turns into a definite resolve, making the action inevitable unless something occurs to prevent it. That is why it is said that steadfastness in respect of lowering the eyes is much easier than the steadfastness needed to endure the pain that results from not doing so. It is an aspect of Allah's kindness to us. He simply forbids us the first step in order to save us from the multitude of afflictions which would follow.

So guard your glance, my brother Muslim, and hold fast to the teachings of your *deen,* and you will save yourself many regrets and sighs and much pain. O Allah, preserve us and grant us Your good pleasure and let us follow Your path, being free from every ailment.

2: The prohibition of all that leads to temptation and enticement

Allah Almighty made it obligatory for Muslim woman to wear the *hijab* to protect the virtue of men whose glances might fall on them and lessen the enticement and temptation they might feel which could stimulate their lower appetites and sexual instinct. As we have already said, it is the strongest of all the instincts and subduing it takes a lot of effort. This aim is helped when the windows onto temptation are closed and women adhere to the teachings of the *Shari'a.* Islam desires to direct human faculties to the service of Muslim society and bring it benefit and ease. Wasting these faculties in cycles of provocation and suppression, of desire and deprivation, of sighs and torments is what the wise *Shari'a* precludes because human faculties are the most precious thing in existence and should be steered in the healthy direction which Allah has ordained for the nurturing of society and establishing the principles of truth and justice.

This is why Islam forbids women to do anything that will lead to temptation and enticement not only in respect of their manner of

26

dressing but also in respect of their manner of speaking and walking. It also forbids their going out and being alone with unrelated men. It is related that 'A'isha, may Allah be pleased with her, said, "Once when the Messenger of Allah, may Allah bless him and grant him peace, was sitting in the mosque, a woman of Muzayna entered the mosque dolled-up in her finery. The Prophet said, 'O people, forbid your women to wear adornments and strut in the mosque. The Children of Israel were not cursed until their women dolled themselves up and strutted in the synagogues." Ibn Maja related it.

'Uqba ibn 'Amir, may Allah be pleased with him, said that the Messenger of Allah, may Allah bless him and grant him peace, said, "Beware of visiting women." A man of the Ansar said, "What about in-laws?" He said, "In-laws are death." By this he meant that the danger in their case is even greater. The evil arising from visiting them and the temptation is greater because it is possible to visit such a woman and be alone with her without any objection being made.

Ibn 'Abbas, may Allah be pleased with him, said that the Messenger of Allah, may Allah bless him and grant him peace, said, "None of you should be alone with a woman unless there is a close relative of hers present (*dhu mahram*)."

It is related from Abu Umama, may Allah be pleased with him, that the Messenger of Allah, may Allah bless him and grant him peace, said, "Beware of being alone with women. By the One who has my soul in His hand, a man is never alone with a woman without Shaytan coming between them. It is better for a man to press up against a pig covered with filth than for his shoulder to press against the shoulder of a woman not lawful for him."

Ma'qil ibn Yasar, may Allah be pleased with him, related that the Messenger of Allah, may Allah bless him and grant him peace, said, "It would be better for one of you to be pierced in the head with an iron prong than to touch a woman not lawful to him."

For this reason Islam forbids a woman to put on perfume and scent when leaving her house in case men smell her perfume. The Prophet, may Allah bless him and grant him peace, said, "Every eye fornicates. When a woman puts on scent and walks past a gathering, she is like so-and-so," meaning a fornicator.

Abu Hurayra, may Allah be pleased with him, related that he met a woman and smelt the fragrance of perfume coming from her and the hem of her dress was raising dust. He said, "Amatu'l-Jabbar! Have you come from the mosque?" She said, "Yes." He said to her, "Did you put on perfume?" She said, "Yes." He said, "I heard Abu'l-Qasim, may Allah bless him and grant him peace, say, 'Allah does not accept the prayer of a woman who puts on perfume before going to the mosque until she has returned and washed it off as she washes for sexual defilement.'"

It is possible to summarise this subject with the words of the Prophet relayed to us by Abu Sa'id, may Allah be pleased with him. He said that the Messenger of Allah, may Allah bless him and grant him peace, said, "Every morning two angels call out: 'Woe to men from women. Woe to women from men.'"

Indeed in the life of a man, there is no more dangerous worldly test for a man than woman and the reverse is also true. That is because in almost every other case the sins which Allah has forbidden to human beings have no natural affinity with them. Injustice in all its forms is unlawful and man is helped to avoid them because human nature is averse to them. Drinking wine is unlawful and it is an easy matter to forbid it as basic human nature is averse to it. The same applies to theft, fraud and slander and the all the other forbidden things which are not in harmony with the laws of nature. However, the sexual instinct is there in every man and woman.

Even though it can drive a person to commit what is unlawful and is considered the pinnacle of dangers in the *Shari'a*, it is nevertheless considered one of the most natural urges of human nature and the most important of its needs, so long as it is reined in by the bridle of the *Shari'a*. There is no way for any healthy human being to separate himself from it or arise above it. This makes it clear to us that sexual appetite is the most dangerous test of a man's *deen* in his life. That is why the Islamic remedy for all other acts of disobedience consists basically in distancing oneself from them and rising above them, whereas in the case of sexuality the remedy lies in satisfying it and enjoying it, but within specific prescribed limits which may not be overstepped.

3: Marriage

Marriage is the basic remedy for the sexual appetite. Alternative solutions are merely to enable you to bide your time until the proper circumstances for marriage arrive: maturity, adequate financial resources, and a virtuous woman. The Messenger of Allah, may Allah bless him and grant him peace, said, "O young men! Any of you who are able to marry should do so. It lowers the eyes and protects the private parts. Any of you who are unable to do so should fast. Fasting is a protection for you." Young men are addressed because they have strength and youthful vigour. They are subject to sexual desire for women and are generally not free of it. An-Nawawi said, "My companions consider the term 'young men' to cover all those who are between the age of puberty and thirty years old." The Prophet prescribed marriage for those who have the means for it and that those who do not have the means should fast and control their desires until the time Allah opens the way for them. We find the source of this in the Noble Qur'an where the Almighty says:

"*Any of you who do not have the means to marry believing free women may marry believing slavegirls who are owned by those among you. Allah knows best about your belief - you are all equally believers. Marry them with their owners' permission and give them their dowries correctly and courteously as married women, not in fornication or taking them as lovers. When they are married, if they commit fornication, they should receive half the punishment of free women. This is for those of you who are afraid of committing fornication. But to be patient would be better for you. Allah is All-Forgiving, Most Merciful.*" (4:25)

This is a dispensation from Allah and a mercy for those Muslims who lack the financial resources to marry believing free women. He therefore unlocks another door for them, but He still concludes by saying, "*But to be patient would be better for you,*" since marriage to slave-girls entails risks in respect of the upbringing of the children which result from it. Islam desires strong progeny who will grow up with dignity, honour and clear lineage and establish Muslim society on firm foundations. That is why the basis of all marriages must be thoroughly sound. Otherwise, it is better to be patient with your sexual desire and to remain abstinent, a policy endorsed by Allah in *Surat an-Nur* when He says:

"Those who cannot find the means to marry should be abstinent until Allah enriches them from His unbounded favour." (24:33)

This call for abstinence and purity is only demanded when a man does not possess adequate financial means to marry. However, when he has the means, marriage becomes an obligatory duty in the *Shari'a*. Listen to the guidance of the noble Prophet regarding the necessity and importance of marriage. It is related from Anas ibn Malik, may Allah be pleased with him, that he heard the Messenger of Allah, may Allah bless him and grant him peace, say, "Whoever wants to meet Allah pure and purified should marry free women."

Abu Ayyub, may Allah be pleased with him, said that the Messenger of Allah, may Allah bless him and grant him peace, said, "Four things are part of the *sunan* of the Messengers: henna, perfume, *siwak*, and marriage."

'Abdullah ibn 'Amr ibn al-'As, may Allah be pleased with both of them, said that the Messenger of Allah, may Allah bless him and grant him peace, said, "This world is passing enjoyment. One of the best kinds of provision it contains is a woman who helps her husband regarding the Next World. A poor man is one who has no wife and a poor woman is one who has no husband."

Abu Umama, may Allah be pleased with him, said that the Prophet, may Allah bless him and grant him peace, said, "There is nothing more beneficial to a believer after fear of Allah Almighty than a virtuous wife. When he orders her to do something, she obeys. When he looks at her, she delights him. When he requests her to do something, she carries it out. When he is absent from her, she is faithful to him both in respect of herself and his property."

Anas, may Allah be pleased with him, related that the Prophet, may Allah bless him and grant him peace, said, "Any man whom Allah provides with a virtuous wife has been helped to half his *deen*, so he should fear Allah regarding the other half."

Abu Hurayra, may Allah be pleased with him, related that the Prophet, may Allah bless him and grant him peace, said, "There are three people whom it is mandatory for Allah to help: someone who does jihad in the way of Allah, a slave who has been given a contract to free himself and desires to fulfil it, and someone who marries out of the desire to preserve his chastity."

Abu Buhayh, may Allah be pleased with him, related that the Prophet, may Allah bless him and grant him peace, said, "Whoever is affluent should marry. If he does not marry, he is not with me."

Anas ibn Malik, may Allah be pleased with him, said, "A group of people came to the houses of the wives of the Prophet, may Allah bless him and grant him peace, to ask about the worship of the Prophet. When they were told, it seemed that they thought that the amount was not sufficient. They said, 'Where are we in relation to the Prophet? Allah has forgiven him his past and future errors.' One of them declared, 'As for myself, I will pray all night.' Another said, 'I will fast continually and never break it.' Another said, 'I will withdraw from women and never marry.' The Messenger of Allah, may Allah bless him and grant him peace, came to them and said, 'Are you the people who said such-and-such? By Allah, I have more fear of Allah than you and more awareness of Him, but I fast and break the fast, and sleep, and marry women. Anyone who is averse to my *Sunna* is not with me.'"

The importance of marriage in Islam

The reasons for the immense importance held by marriage in the life of the Muslims are summarised in the following points:

- It is obedience to the command of Allah, who says in the Qur'an: *"Marry those among you who are unmarried and*

31

your slaves and slavegirls who are righteous. If they are poor Allah will enrich them from His overflowing favour." (24:32)

- It is following the guidance of our beloved Prophet and all the Messengers of Allah since Allah Almighty says in His description and praise of the Messengers: *"We sent Messengers before you and gave them wives and children too"* (13:38). An aspect of Allah's love for the human race lies in enabling them to have children to perpetuate the human species. The child is the goal of both the legal contract and the physical pleasure it sanctions. However, there is no pleasure in the life of the Muslim which does not entail subsequent responsibility, as is shown in this case by the upbringing of children.

- It gives repose and delight to the soul since sitting with, looking at, and playing with one's spouse allows the heart to relax and strengthens it for worship. Without this the soul would grow wearied and turn away from the truth. The Almighty says: *"Among His signs is that He created for you spouses from yourselves so that you might find repose with them. And He has placed between you affection and mercy. In that there are certainly signs for people who reflect"* (30:21).

- It fortifies the heart against Shaytan by satisfying sexual desire and therefore averting the dangers of the unbridled sexual appetite. It is like an impregnable fortress which protects the Muslims from fornication and so saves them from falling into the abyss which plunges people into the lower levels of Hellfire in this world before the Next. There is no more effective way of dealing with sexual energy.

- It frees the heart from the worldly preoccupations which result from the promptings of passion and sexual desire, leaving it free for other-worldly aspirations. The Prophet, may Allah bless him and grant him peace, said, "There is nothing like marriage for two people who love one another."

32

- It provides an arena for combating and disciplining the lower self through taking care of the family and looking after their needs, putting up with their faults and failings, and striving to bring them up well and guide them to the right path. The Prophet, may Allah bless him and grant him peace, said, "What a man spends on his family is *sadaqa*." He said, "A man is rewarded for the mouthful he gives to his wife."

Truly man should be amazed at the wisdom of the way his Lord deals with the sexual instinct. It allows the sexual appetite to be satisfied, provides man with progeny and encourages him to strive on behalf of his family. Every aspect of the human self is taken into account and the result is a pure fruit whose fragrance permeates all parts of Muslim society. Muslims are encouraged to satisfy their sexual instinct and by doing so achieve good in this world and the Next. This made the leaders among the Companions and the Followers as eager to marry as they were to please Allah and His Messenger. 'Umar, may Allah be pleased with him, said, "I force myself to have sexual intercourse hoping that Allah will bring forth by means of it another human being to glorify and remember Him."

Ibn Mas'ud, may Allah be pleased with him, said, "Even if only ten days of my life remained, I would still get married because I would not like to meet Allah unmarried." He also said, "Seek wealth through marriage in conformity with the words of Allah, *'If they are poor Allah will enrich them from His overflowing favour'* (24:32)".

Imam Ahmad ibn Hanbal said, "Anyone who calls on you not to marry has called you to something other than Islam." He, may Allah have mercy on him, married two days after the death of his wife and said, "I do not want to spend a night as an unmarried man."

4. Treating the sexual organs through the stomach

Since food is the body's basic fuel by which the movement of the various limbs and all the life functions of man are achieved, a little food is clearly necessary for the continuance of life. The Prophet, may Allah bless him and grant him peace, said, "A human being does not fill any vessel worse than his stomach. Enough for the son of Adam are a few morsels to keep his back straight. If it cannot be avoided, then a third is for food, a third for drink, and a third for breath." He also said, "We are a people who do not eat until we are hungry and when we do eat, do not eat our fill."

This is the exemplary method which Islam has prescribed with admirable succinctness to obtain the best result: we should not eat until we are hungry and when we do eat, we should not eat our fill: a third for food, a third for drink, and a third for breath.

Why is Islam concerned with encouraging Muslims to eat only a little? The answer shows the greatness of Islam in fashioning the human mind and soul. More food entails an increase in the blood which flows through the body and this, in turn, entails greater opportunities for Shaytan, allowing him to attack and move in his field of action, awakening the appetites from their dormant state and unleashing the desires of the lower self. This causes man to gravitate to the earth, indulging his lower appetites and nurturing his body with the material things of life. This deadens the intelligence and causes the spirit to sink to its lowest possibility. This is a clear state of loss.

That is why the natural *Shari'a* prescribes curbing the appetite for food because it is the widest path to stimulating the desires of the sexual organs. That is why the Prophet instructed young men to fast when they are unable to marry. The description of the believer is linked to little food. Gluttony, greed and large quantities of food are the attributes of the unbeliever as the Almighty says:

"Those who reject will have their enjoyment, eating as cattle eat, but the Fire will be their residence." (47:12)

The Messenger of Allah, may Allah bless him and grant him peace, said, "A Muslim eats in one intestine and an unbeliever in seven intestines." An-Nawawi explained this *hadith* by saying, "The seven attributes of the unbeliever are avarice, gluttony, excessive expectation, bad nature, envy and love of obesity." Al-

34

Qurtubi said, "There are seven appetites for food: the appetite of nature, the appetite of the lower self, the appetite of the eye, the appetite of the mouth, the appetite of the ear, the appetite of the nose and the appetite of hunger. The last is the necessary one by which the believer eats."

Ibn at-Tin said, "People are in three categories in respect of food. One group eats every kind of food, necessary and superfluous. This is the behaviour of the people of the *Jahiliyya*. Another group eats what will allay hunger when they are hungry. Another group make themselves hungry, intending by that to curb the appetite of the self. When they eat, they eat enough to keep themselves alive."

If you give your stomach everything it wants,
    your genitals will incur the utmost reprimand.

Listen, my Muslim brother, to the words of Allah Almighty:

"You dissipated the good things you had in your worldly life and enjoyed yourself in it. Therefore today you are being repaid with the punishment of humiliation." (46:20)

This admonishes those who are engrossed in permitted good things, because whoever accustoms himself to that becomes predisposed to this world. He is not safe from being in thrall to his appetites and to sensual pleasures. Whenever he indulges in one of them, his lower self calls him to another. This continues until he cannot control the rebelliousness of his lower self at all and the door of worship becomes closed to him. He must not allow his lower self to become so accustomed to gluttony that it becomes difficult to correct it. The stomach is the root of all sickness.

That is why the guidance of the Prophet involved giving clear directions leading to balance in respect of food and urging restraint of that appetite which provides fuel for the more dangerous sexual appetite.

Anas ibn Malik, may Allah be pleased with him, related that the Messenger of Allah, may Allah bless him and grant him peace, said, "One aspect of profligacy is eating everything you desire."

35

'A'isha, may Allah be pleased with her, said, "One day the Messenger of Allah, may Allah bless him and grant him peace, saw me eat twice. He said, ''A'isha, do you make filling your stomach your sole occupation? Eating twice a day is one aspect of profligacy. Allah does not love the profligate.'"

It is related that 'A'isha said, "The first disaster which occurred to this community after its Prophet died was satiety. When people fill their stomachs, their bodies become fat, their hearts weak and their appetites ingrained."

It is related that 'Atiyya ibn 'Amir al-Juhani said that he heard Salman say when he was forced to eat some food, "It is enough for me that I heard the Messenger of Allah, may Allah bless him and grant him peace, say, 'The people who fill themselves the most in this world will be the hungriest on the Day of Rising ''"

It is related from Abu Hurayra that the Messenger of Allah, may Allah bless him and grant him peace, said, "On the Day of Rising, a huge tall man who ate and drank to excess will come and in Allah's sight he will weigh no more than a gnat's wing. If you wish, recite: 'We will not give them any weight on the Day of Resurrection' (18:105)."

Ibn Bujayr, one of the Companions, said, "The Prophet, may Allah bless him and grant him peace, felt hungry one day. He took a stone and tied it against his stomach and then said, 'Those who eat well and are comfortable in this world will be hungry and naked on the Day of Rising. Anyone who is generous to his lower self will be humbled before it. Anyone who humbles his lower self is being generous to it."

Mu'adh ibn Jabal, may Allah be pleased with him, related that when the Messenger of Allah, may Allah bless him and grant him peace, sent him to Yemen, he said to him, "Beware of comfort. The slaves of Allah do not make themselves comfortable."

It is related from Abu Umama that the Messenger of Allah, may Allah bless him and grant him peace, said, "There will be men of my community who consume diverse kinds of food and diverse kinds of drink, wear diverse kinds of clothing and speak in an affected way. They are the worst of my community."

Ad-Dahhak ibn Sufyan related that the Messenger of Allah, may Allah bless him and grant him peace, said to him, "Dahhak, what does your food consist of?" He said, "Meat and milk, Messenger of Allah." He said, "Then what does it turn into?" He said, "You know what it turns into." He said, "Allah Almighty has made what is excreted by the son of Adam a metaphor for this world."

From these illuminating *hadiths* of the Prophet it should be clear to us that hunger is a river from which the angels drink and satiety is an ocean from which Shaytan drinks. Whoever guards his stomach also guards his genitals. There must first be control over the appetite of the stomach in order for there to be control over the sexual appetite. Base matter is the fuel of Hellfire but the origin of the spirit is pure light. Islam is concerned firstly with the spirit and giving it its provision from the luminosity of the Qur'an and worship and righteous actions. In the case of the body, the commands of Islam make sure it is confined within the firm stockade of contentment, chastity, and purity. One righteous man said, "Do not be led astray by the words of the Almighty, *'Eat and drink.'* The outward meaning of the *ayat* is honouring and giving enjoyment. But inwardly it is a test and trial so that He can see who is with Him and who is simply self-indulgent."

Allah Almighty revealed to Da'ud, peace be upon him: "I created the lower appetites for the weak of My creation. Beware of letting your heart become attached to any of your appetites. Anything you might suffer by heeding this warning is far easier than having the sweetness of My love stripped from your heart. O Da'ud, cling to My words and take from yourself for yourself. Do not ignore them so that I veil My love from you. Deny your appetite for My sake. I allow appetites to the weak of My creation. I ask the strong to disparage their appetites. They diminish the sweetness of conversation with Me. I am not content with this world for those I love, and I strip it from them. O Da'ud, do not put between Me and you a drunken sage whose love will veil you from My love by his intoxication. Such people block the path for the weak among My slaves. Seek help in abandoning your appetites by devotion to fasting. O Da'ud, you should prefer to oppose your lower self and deny it its appetites. If you do you will see the veils between Me and you lifted."

O Allah! Provide us with contentment and help us to fast and oppose our lower selves. Let us avoid gluttony, coarseness, and greediness! Make our food enough for us as You did for the Master of Creation and the Beloved of the Truth!

5. The correct behaviour to be observed when entering people's homes

Homes are secure places and protected fortresses where a woman is permitted to remove her outer covering because, as the Prophet said, "Any woman who removes her garment outside her house has sundered what is between her and Allah." Women should be able to carry out their household tasks safe from the prying eyes of uninvited guests without needing to veil themselves. Islam strongly encourages that freedom in which a woman lives inside the house and protects her purity, chastity and modesty from being disturbed by the unexpected glance; it therefore establishes regulations and limits with regard to entering private houses. This is to ensure that no temptation occurs between men and women the results of which may be blameworthy. It is so easy for the urges of appetite to be provoked, leading to the ensuing desires against which the *Shari'a* so strongly cautions. This is why the places of ambush should be shut off and the entrances by which Shaytan travels to man blocked up. The Almighty says in His Noble Book:

"O you who believe! Do not enter houses other than your own until you have asked permission and greeted their inhabitants. That is better for you - so that perhaps you will remember. And if you find no one at home do not go in until permission has been granted you. And if you are told to go away then go away. That is far purer for you. Allah knows what you do. There is no blame on you for entering houses where no one lives and where there is advantage for you. Allah knows what you make known and all that you conceal." (24:27-28)

38

From the explanation of these *ayats* and the *hadiths* of the Prophet, may Allah bless him and grant him peace, we can deduce that the correct behaviour regarding entering private houses has the following clear principles:

• A believer must ask permission to enter other people's homes. This precaution is even more important if the house belongs to someone who is not one of his relatives. He should say, "Peace be upon you" three times. If he is given permission to go in, he may enter. Otherwise he should go away - in fact it is obligatory for him to go away.

• Lack of permission to enter can be explicit or implicit, like silence. A believer must not be angry at being refused permission.

• When a believer asks permission to enter, he should not stand directly in front of the door but to one side of it. He must clearly state his name or the name by which he is known and not just say, "It's me."

• A believer should also ask permission from his mother and sister, because he does not want to see them naked. In the case of his wife, he is not obliged to ask permission but it is recommended for him to do so since she might well be in a state in which she would not like her husband to see her.

• As for houses which are not private homes, such as hotels, inns and similar places, there is no harm in entering them without permission.

The *ayats* which were quoted above are a protection and safeguard for all believers. So every believer should find that others guard his inviolable things as he guards theirs. The Messenger of Allah, may Allah bless him and grant him peace, spoke the truth when he said, "Every eye will weep on the Day of Rising except an eye which has been restrained from looking at the things Allah has prohibited, an eye which has been sleepless in the way of Allah, and an eye which has wept itself dry out of fear of Allah Almighty."

O Messenger of Allah, you spoke the truth. Restraining the eyes from looking at the things Allah has prohibited protects Muslims from slipping into disobedience to Allah. If that happens all the tears in this world and a whole lifetime will not be sufficient regret for what has been neglected in respect of Allah.

O Allah, protect our eyes, ears, and limbs from disobedience to You and connect our hearts to You and confine our aspirations to You! You are the Merciful, the Compassionate, the Generous, the Noble.

6. The prohibition against pursuing desires

Appetite is the impulse of the self to follow the paths of desire and pursuit of desire is a path that leads to Hellfire. Its danger is such that Allah cautioned His worshipping servant Da'ud:

"O Da'ud! We made you a khalif in the earth. So judge between people with truth and do not pursue whims and desires and let them lead you astray from Allah's way. Those who go astray from Allah's way will receive harsh punishment for their forgetting the Day of Reckoning."
(38:26)

Da'ud used to fast every other day. The Master of the Prophets, Muhammad, may Allah bless him and grant him peace, said about him, "The best of fasts is the fast of Da'ud. He used to fast one day and break the fast one day. The best night prayers are those of Da'ud. He used to sleep half the night and then pray a third and then sleep a sixth." This is a statement issuing from the trustworthy truthful one to whom his Lord said:

"Be steadfast in the face of what they say, and remember Our slave Da'ud, possessor of strength. He truly turned towards his Lord." (38:17)

Moreover Allah cautioned him as well against pursuing desire because it leads one away from the Path of Allah:

"And who could be further astray than someone who follows his own whims and desires without any guidance from Allah? Allah does not guide the people of the wrong-doers." (28:50)

Desire means gravitating to the earth and inclining to the lower appetites and neglecting Allah's remembrance. That is misguidance itself - we seek refuge with Allah! - and destruction in the lowest levels of Hellfire. For this reason a believer is asked to strive against the desires of his lower self because it is the precursor of fornication. Allah made the repayment for that striving the Garden of Refuge:

"But as for him who fears the Station of his Lord and forbids the self its appetites, the Garden is his refuge."
(79:39-40)

Resistance to the impulses of desire is the result of fear of Allah. It is said that the only way for appetite to leave the heart is through an unsettling fear or restless yearning. So fear of Allah's punishment and yearning to meet Him are the two things which cleanse the heart of the indulgence of appetites. In view of the tremendous value of fear of Allah which only arises from great knowledge and an awakened heart and an illuminated reproachful self, Allah has made the repayment commensurably enormous:

"He who feared the Station of his Lord will have two Gardens." (55:46)

O Allah, we praise You and thank You for Your bounty and generosity. You summon us to free ourselves from slavehood to our appetites and then are generous to us and give us for doing it the generous gift of two Gardens.

My brother Muslim, you must oppose the stirrings of desire when they are first aroused because they foreshadow the release of the sexual appetite from its leash, your entry into the thraldom of slavehood to material existence, and your being stripped of Allah's veil with which He veils you when you are in the arena of belief:

Many a veiled one, captive to by his appetite,
is stripped of his veil and disgraced.
He who is possessed by desire is a slave.
He who masters his desires becomes a king.

7. The use of the intellect as a means to subdue the appetites

It is related that when the husband of Rabi'a al-'Adawiyya died, al-Hasan al-Basri and his companions asked for permission to visit her. She gave them permission to come in and let down a curtain and sat behind it. Al-Hasan and his companions said,

"Your husband has died. You should have someone to replace him."

"All right," she said, "but which of you has the most knowledge, so that I can marry him?"

"Al-Hasan al-Basri," they replied.

"If you can answer me four questions, I am yours," she said to al-Hasan.

"Ask," said al-Hasan. "If Allah gives me success, I will answer them for you."

"What do you say to this," she asked. "when I die and leave this world, will I leave with belief or not?"

"That is a matter of the Unseen and none knows the Unseen except Allah."

"What about this, then? When I am put into the grave and Munkar and Nakir question me, will I be able to answer them or not?"

"That is a matter of the Unseen and none knows the Unseen except Allah," replied al-Hasan a second time.

"When people are gathered together on the Day of Rising and the books are distributed, will I be given my book in my right hand or my left hand?"

"That too is a matter of the Unseen and none knows the Unseen except Allah," came the reply again.

"When people are called: 'One group in the Garden and one group in the Blaze!' which of the two groups will I be in?"

"That is a matter of the Unseen and none knows the Unseen except Allah," responded al-Hasan for the fourth and last time.

"How is it possible," she retorted, "for someone who is suffering the grief of ignorance about these four things to think of marriage?"

"O Hasan," she continued, "in how many parts did Allah create the intellect?"

"In ten parts," he replied, "nine for men and one for women."

"O Hasan, in how many parts did Allah create appetite?"

"In ten parts: nine for women and one for men."

"O Hasan," she concluded, "I am able to contain nine parts of appetite with one part of intellect whereas you cannot even guard one part of appetite with nine parts of intellect!" Thereupon al-Hasan wept and left her.

Because of its ability to keep the appetites in check, Islam is very much concerned with the intellect, nurturing it, developing it and giving it the greatest scope to evaluate things and their results with precise criteria. It should be used to distinguish the positive and negative sides of appetite using the criterion of the *Shari'a* and to understand what its consequences will be in this world and the Next. It should know how to encourage the lower self to gain the pleasure of Allah and how to make it wary of the anger of Allah so that it does not collapse under the pressure of impulses, appetites and desires and become lost in the oceans of this world. Out of His endless generosity the Almighty has prescribed various measures to safeguard the intellect and promote the development and expansion of its faculties.

Among these measures is Revelation itself. One of the functions of Revelation and the Message is to act as Allah's evidence against mankind. Left to itself, the intellect can misguide. Natural form (*fitra*) on its own is also capable of deviation. The only safe-guard for the intellect and natural form is to adopt the Revelation as their directing guide:

"We never punish until We have sent a Messenger."
(17:15)

Therefore the intellect needs the Revelation to guide it and direct it and make it sound so that it can distinguish the bad from the good. Revelation protects the intellect from becoming lost in materialistic philosophies.

Another of the safeguards of the intellect is the prohibition of intoxicants. Many a man fritters away his intellectual abilities in satisfying his lower appetites and passing whims and this opens him up to misguidance, deviation and bad habits of all kinds which will disrupt first his own life, then the life of his family, and finally that of society as a whole. This is the root cause of Islam's prohibition of intoxicants of all sorts - alcohol, drugs, or any substance that has an effect on the brain, leading to altered states of consciousness or hallucinations. The Almighty says in His Noble Book:

"O you who believe! Wine and gambling and stone altars and divining arrows are disgusting things, part of the handiwork of Shaytan. Avoid them completely, so that perhaps you will be successful." (5:90)

Could there be any greater accomplishment than being awake and alert and perceiving where your steps are taking you and being able to truly evaluate their prospective benefit or harm for yourself in this world and the Next?

Another thing which Allah does in this respect is to invite the intellect to reflect deeply on existence. The purpose of this invitation is to free the intellect of the chains that shackle it and make it stumble under the pressure of all the needs and demands which hem it in. When man contemplates the universe, he is inevitably aware of the immensity of its Creator and His strength and this impels him to seek help and strength from Him to undertake the task for which he was created. Such contemplation awakens him

44

from the sleep of heedlessness and opens all his receptive senses and cognitive faculties:

> *"Truly in the creation of the heavens and the earth, and the alternation of night and day there are signs for people of intelligence."* (3:190)

> *"Have they not travelled in the land? Do they not have hearts with which to understand or ears with which to hear?"* (22:46)

In all created existence there is nothing more noble than the human intellect and for this reason Allah honours it as it deserves. There is no *deen* which fulfils all the aspirations of the intellect and answers its questions as Islam does. This is only to be expected since the intellect is the supreme instrument of human perception and whenever it is polished, perception is increased and the results derived from its use are greater. A bedouin possessing an unspoiled natural response to existence articulated this when people asked him, "Why do you believe in Muhammad?" His reply was: "Because what his *deen* orders leaves no scope for the intellect to say, "If only he had ordered this." Nor does what it forbids leave the intellect any scope to say, "If only he had not forbidden that."

This is why we find much repeated in the Qur'an: *"Do they not reflect?" "Will they not then use their understanding?" "In that are signs for a people who believe..., who use their understanding..., who have certainty."*

O Allah, place us among those who listen to Your Word and follow the best of it! Grant us light in our eyes, light in our ears, and light in our intellects! Guide us to the best character and actions. Only You can guide to that.

8. Fear of Allah

Fear of Allah (*taqwa*) is the focal point, buttress and summit of the entire affair. When Allah addresses the wives of the Prophet in *Surat al-Ahzab*, and hence all believing women who have a good model in the Mothers of the Believers, He says: *"...provided you are godfearing. Do not be soft in your speech in case someone with sickness in his heart becomes desirous. Speak correct and courteous words"* (33:32), and the rest of the instructions which encourage purity and chastity.

This shows that fear of Allah is the firm foundation on which all idea of noble character in Muslim society is based. It is the comprehensive principle which upholds the edifice of Islam once its foundations have been established: its obligations and usages. Sayyiduna 'Ali, may Allah be pleased with him, defined it in this way: "It is acting according to the Revelation, fear of the Majestic, contentment with little and making preparation for the Day of Departure." Fear of Allah is therefore the strongest of all weapons.

Sayyiduna 'Umar, may Allah be pleased with him, said, "Fear of Allah means avoidance of everything Allah has forbidden."

One of the righteous said, "Directing oneself to Allah Almighty alone, abandoning the occupations of the body, exercising scrupulousness in all one's actions, and being freed from bondage to the visible world are all results of fear of Allah, as Allah promises when He says: *'Fear Allah and Allah will teach you'* (2:282) and *'Take provision, but the best provision is fear of Allah. Therefore fear Me, people of intelligence!'* (2:197)"

Shah ibn Shuja' al-Kirmani used to say, "Whoever occupies his outward with following the *Sunna* and his inward with constant watchfulness and withholding his eyes from looking at unlawful things and restraining himself from appetites will not have his understanding err. Allah Almighty will repay him for his actions in kind. Whoever abandons something for the sake of Allah, He will give him something better in return. If he restrains his eyes from the things Allah has forbidden him to see, Allah will, in return for his self-restraint, liberate the light of his inner sight. He will open for him the door of knowledge, belief, gnosis, and the true understanding that is only experienced through the heart. The converse of this is the blind wandering that is the opposite of insight and by which Allah characterised the people of Lut: *"By your life, they were wandering blindly in their drunken state!"* (15:72). He describes them as drunk, indicating derangement of the intellect, and blind indicating complete lack of insight. Attachment to created forms causes derangement of the intellect. Lack of insight intoxicates the heart."

O Allah! make it easy for us to follow those You love and make their openings extend to us! Join us to them and gather us in their company and guide us as they were guided and let us travel on their path! Our God and Master! We ask you to put our affairs in order and the destinies of our relatives and those we love. Pour out mercy on us from the sea of Your *ihsan* and mend us with Your forgiveness and slake the thirst of our hearts with Your pleasure. Prescribe Your protection for us, O Lord of the worlds!

The penalty for not safeguarding the private parts

This has been a selection of the luminous indications which the All-Wise Lawgiver has given us to enable us to safeguard our private parts and thereby protect the purity and cohesion of Muslim society so that it may avoid the numerous perils which might otherwise dissipate its energy. What then is the position of Islam *vis-a-vis* the limits which it has prescribed to protect the community? Allah and His Messenger warned all who are tempted to break those limits in the strongest possible fashion and then imposed severe punishments in this world before the Next for any who commit the crime of fornication. This is because most people are only deterred by immediate force and do not give any real weight to the punishments of the Next World. That fact has given rise to the saying: "Allah will curb by the hand of the ruler what is not curbed by the words of the Qur'an."

Listen, my Muslim brother, to Allah's warnings and the punishment for fornication as prescribed in the Noble Qur'an:

"Anyone who disobeys Allah and His Messenger and goes beyond His limits, We will admit him into a Fire, remaining in it timelessly, forever. He will have a humiliating punishment." (4:14)

"Do not go near to fornication. It is an indecent act, an evil way." (17:32)

"Those who do not call on another god together with Allah and do not kill any person Allah has made inviolate - except with a right - and do not fornicate. Anyone who does that will receive an evil punishment." (25:68)

"Your Lord has made it unlawful for you ... to approach indecency - outward or inward." (6:151)

"Allah commands justice and doing good and giving to relatives. And He forbids indecency and doing wrong and tyranny. He warns you so that perhaps you will remember." (16:95)

"If any of your women commit fornication, four of you must appear as witnesses against them. And if witnesses against them do come forward, shut them up in their homes until death comes to them or Allah ordains some other way for them. If two among you do it, castigate both of them. Then if they repent and reform, leave them alone. Allah is Ever-returning, Most Merciful." (4:15-16)

"A woman who fornicates and a man who fornicates, flog each of them one hundred lashes. And do not let compassion for either of them take hold of you where Allah's deen is concerned, if you believe in Allah and the Last Day. And a group of the believers should witness their punishment. A man who fornicates may only marry a woman who fornicates or an idolater. A woman who fornicates may only marry a man who fornicates or an idolater. Such have been forbidden to the believers." (24:2-3)

When we go to the *Sunna* we find nine further aspects of the punishment to be meted out to those who commit the abhorrent crime of fornication or adultery.

1: The removal of the light of belief from the heart

Abu Hurayra, may Allah be pleased with him, said that the Messenger of Allah, may Allah bless him and grant him peace, said, "A fornicator does not fornicate while a believer, a thief does not steal while a believer, and a man does not drink alcohol while a believer. When someone does that, the halter of Islam slips from his neck. If he repents, Allah turns to him."

2: The death penalty for adulterers

'Abdullah ibn Mas'ud, may Allah be pleased with him, said that the Messenger of Allah, may Allah bless him and grant him peace, said, "The blood of a Muslim man who testifies that there is no god but Allah and that I am the Messenger of Allah is not lawful except in three cases: that of a previously married person who fornicates, in the case of a life for a life, and that of someone who abandons his *deen* and leaves the community."

3: The arrival of poverty and anxiety

Ibn 'Umar, may Allah be pleased with him, said that the Messenger of Allah, may Allah bless him and grant him peace, said, "Fornication bequeaths poverty."

'Abdullah ibn Zayd, may Allah be pleased with him, said, "I heard the Prophet, may Allah bless him and grant him peace, say, "O fornicatresses of the Arabs! O fornicatresses of the Arabs! The thing I fear most for you is fornication and hidden lust."

4: Allah's refusal to respond

'Uthman ibn Abi'l-'As said that the Messenger of Allah, may Allah bless him and grant him peace, said, "The gates of heaven are opened in the middle of the night and a caller calls out: 'Is there anyone who calls, that he may be answered? If there anyone who asks, that he may be given? Is there anyone with a grief, that it may be relieved?' There is no Muslim who makes a supplication without Allah Almighty answering him - except for a fornicator or tax-collector."

5: Burnt faces on the Day of Rising

'Abdullah ibn Busr said that the Prophet, may Allah bless him and grant him peace, said, "The faces of fornicators will be burned with fire."

6: Being thrown into an oven

Samura ibn Jundub said that the Prophet, may Allah bless him and grant him peace, said, "In the night I dreamt that two men came to me and took me to a holy land..." In the course of this long *hadith*, he says, "They took me to a hole like a oven whose top was narrow and its bottom wide, under which a fire was burning. When the fire rose, the people in it rose as well until they almost came out; and when it died down, they went back down into it. It contained naked men and women."

7: Erasure from the register of the pious and being expelled from their company

Abu Hurayra said that the Messenger of Allah, may Allah bless him and grant him peace, said, "There are three to whom Allah will not speak on the Day of Rising nor will He declare them innocent or look at them, and they will have a painful punishment: an adulterous old man, a lying king, and an arrogant poor man."

Burayda said that the Messenger of Allah, may Allah bless him and grant him peace, said, "The seven heavens and the seven earths curse an adulterous old man. The smell of the genitals of fornicators is disgusting even to the people of the Fire."

Nafi' said that the Messenger of Allah, may Allah bless him and grant him peace, said, "Neither an arrogant poor man, nor an adulterous old man, nor a person who thinks that Allah owes something him on account of his actions will enter the Garden."

8: Ruined, dissolute and degraded offspring

Maymuna, may Allah be pleased with her, said: "I heard the Messenger of Allah, may Allah bless him and grant him peace, say, "My community will remain sound as long as illegitimate children do not abound among them. When illegitimate children abound, Allah will soon envelop them in punishment."

9: Allah's punishment for society as a whole

Ibn 'Abbas said that the Messenger of Allah, may Allah bless him and grant him peace, said, "When fornication and usury appear in a place, the people there have legitimised Allah's punishment for themselves."

✳✸✳✸✳

Having examined the punishment for fornication in the Noble Qur'an and Prophetic *Sunna*, it is clear that the Muslim should tremble before that outrage because of the immense woes it entails in this world and the Next. What we have outlined in this section should be more than sufficient to ensure the development of every Muslim's conscience, feelings and behaviour and to keep him on the wise path of Allah and the upright *Shari'a*. This will enable the Muslims to create an Islamic society built on the firm foundations of Truth and not on diverse desires and impulses which will only serve to drag them down into the depths of Hellfire.

We bear witness to Your Greatness, o Lord, and Your Wisdom. You created the illness and prescribed the cure. You created instincts in man and along with them You created laws and rules which provide a strong bulwark against the unleashing of their destructive power. In fact, You refined them, polished them and directed them by means of the sound *Shari'a* so as to achieve life and success for Islamic society.

We bear witness, O Lord, to the greatness of Your Messenger in conveying Your message and taking the hands of the Muslims with mercy and compassion to lead them to the pathways of light so that they are able to strive against the urges of their lower selves and base appetites. The nourishment of the spirit and intellect is belief in Allah and His Angels and His Books and His Messengers and the Decree of good and evil. This belief will refine them and give them control over the appetites in a manner that is pleasing to Allah and His Messenger.

When one of the Muslims came to Allah's Messenger asking him to permit him to commit fornication, he did not attack him directly and slam the doors of mercy in his face. Rather he strengthened his heart for him and dealt gently with him. He asked him if he would be pleased for his wife or his mother or his sister to do such a thing. In each case the man said no and found it repre-

51

hensible in the case of his family. In this way the Messenger, may Allah bless him and grant him peace, made him understand and prayed to Allah to remove the intensity of desire for women from his breast. The man got up and found that Allah had cured him by the guidance of belief and the alertness of his intellect.

O Allah, guide us by Your noble guidance and illuminate our insight and intellects with the light of faith and certainty so that we are able to see the Truth as truth and follow it and see the false as false and avoid it.

Chaper Three
The Remedy for Excessive Love of Children

The importance of love of children

Love of children is a natural instinct in parents. It is a great blessing for us from Allah since if it were not for that love the human species would become extinct. Parents show endless patience in caring for their children and providing for them and bringing them up. They spend many sleepless nights for their children's sake and deny themselves many things in order to look after their best interests, finding sweetness in even the most severe difficulties they undergo on their behalf. The Noble Qur'an describes these noble true parental feelings in the most delightful manner in a number of clear *ayats*. Sometimes Allah speaks of children as an adornment and one of the glories of this life:

"Wealth and sons are the embellishment of the life of this world." (18:46)

At other times He regards them as an immense blessing for which gratitude must be shown to the Giver and Blesser:

"We fortified you with wealth and children and made you greater in number." (17:6)

Another time He deems them a delight, provided they follow the path of the godfearing:

"Those who say, 'Our Lord, give us delight in our wives and our children, and make us a good example for the godfearing.'" (25:74)

Children are a great boon gained by the blessing of asking forgiveness and entreating Allah:

"I said, 'Ask forgiveness of your Lord. Truly He is Endlessly Forgiving. He will send heaven down on you in copious rain and fortify you with more wealth and sons, and grant you gardens and grant you waterways.'"
(71:10-12)

The Messengers call on people to fear Allah and obey Him in return for the children they have been given:

"Fear Him who has sustained you in ways you know about, sustained you with pasturing animals and children, and with gardens and clear springs." (26:132-134)

Allah also makes them the ultimate divine gift, the good news and answer to the supplication of His Prophets:

"There and then Zakariyya called on his Lord, and said, 'O Lord, grant me, from Yourself, an upright descendant. You are the Hearer of prayer.' The angels called out to him while he was standing in prayer in the Upper Room, 'Allah gives you the good news of Yahya, who will come to confirm a Word from Allah, and will be a leader and a celibate, a Prophet, and one of the righteous.' He said, 'My Lord, how can I possibly have a son when I have reached old age and my wife is barren?' He said, 'It shall be so. Allah does whatever He wills.'" (3:38-40)

"When the angels said, 'Maryam! Your Lord gives you the good news of a Word from Him. His name is the Messiah, 'Isa son of Maryam, of high esteem in this world and the Next World, one of those brought near. He will

speak to people in the cradle and also when fully grown, and he will be one of the righteous.' She said, 'My Lord! How can I possibly have a son when no man has ever touched me?' He said, 'It shall be so. Allah creates anything He wills. When He decides on something, He just says to it, 'Be!' and it is." (3:45-47)

"He said, 'I am going towards my Lord. He will guide me. My Lord, give me a righteous child!' We gave him the good news of an intelligent lad." (37:99-101)

"His wife was standing there and laughed. So We gave her the good news of Ishaq, and beyond Ishaq, Ya'qub. She said, 'Woe is me! Am I to give birth when I am an old woman and my husband here is an old man? This is indeed an amazing thing!' They said, 'Are you amazed by the Command of Allah? May the mercy of Allah and His blessings be upon you, O people of the House! He is Praiseworthy, Glorious.'" (11:70-72)

It is no wonder that the term "good news" is always used in respect of the divine gift of children. Children are a natural help to man both in his life and after his death. They are the candles which illuminate his life and give it meaning and value. They are the worldly seedbed which enables him to enter the Garden provided he tends them well and waters them with the teachings of Allah and His Messenger. He produces from them men who will carry the banner of truth fluttering high and women who will undertake the rearing of their children with love of Allah and His Messenger.

See, then, the supreme importance of the part played by offspring in human life. The wise Lawgiver is concerned with their care and safeguarding them and teaching them what is pleasing to Allah and His Messenger.

Mercy to children is a gift from Allah to His slaves

Among the noble feelings which Allah has placed in the hearts of parents is a feeling of mercy towards children, compassion for them and kindness to them. It is a noble feeling which helps parents to endure hardship and expend effort for the sake of bringing up a new generation of Muslims. Someone whose heart is bereft of the quality of mercy is described as gruff and harsh. This is not the character of a true Muslim who follows the path of the Prophet of Mercy, the one whom Allah sent as a "mercy to all the worlds", the one who said about mercy, "He who has no mercy will not be shown mercy."

Mercy is a radiant light which helps people to restrain their rancour and forgive others, to have kindness, gentleness and forbearance, and to pardon wrong and maintain ties even with those who break them. This is why the Messenger, may Allah bless him and grant him peace, was so concerned with mercy and why he encouraged people to take on this noble characteristic, for it is a spreading tree which shades the weak from the heat and ferocity of life.

'Amr ibn Shu'ayb, may Allah be pleased with him, related that the Messenger of Allah, may Allah bless him and grant him peace, said, "Anyone who does not show mercy to our young people or acknowledge the rights of our old people is not one of us."

Abu Hurayra, may Allah be pleased with him, said, "A man with a child came to the Prophet, may Allah bless him and grant him peace, and began to hug the child warmly. The Prophet said, 'Do you feel mercy for him?' He replied, 'Yes.' The Prophet said, 'Allah is more merciful to you than you are to him. He is the Most Merciful of the Merciful.'"

'A'isha, may Allah be pleased with her, said, "A bedouin came to the Prophet, may Allah bless him and grant him peace, and said, 'Do you kiss your children? We do not kiss ours.' The Prophet said, 'Can I help it if Allah has removed mercy from your heart?'"

Anas ibn Malik said, "A woman [with two daughters] came to 'A'isha and 'A'isha gave her three dates. She gave each of her daughters a date and kept one for herself. The children ate the two dates and looked at their mother; the mother took her date and split it in two and gave each child half of it. The Prophet, may Allah bless him and grant him peace, came and 'A'isha told him what had happened. He said, 'Why are you surprised at that? Allah will show mercy to her on account of her mercy to her children.'"

Usama ibn Zayd reported: "The daughter of the Prophet, may Allah bless him and grant him peace, sent word to her father that her son was dying, asking him to come. He sent his greetings and said, 'Allah takes what is His and what He gives is also His. Everything has a fixed term with Him, so she should show fortitude and expect a reward.' She sent to him adjuring him to come to her. So he got up with Sa'd ibn 'Ubada, Mu'adh ibn Jabal, Ubayy ibn Ka'b, Zayd ibn Thabit and some other men, may Allah be pleased with them. The child was brought to the Messenger of Allah, may Allah bless him and grant him peace. He laid him in his lap and he was shuddering. The Prophet's eyes were flowing with tears. Sa'd asked, 'Messenger of Allah, what is this?' He said, 'This is an aspect of mercy which Allah Almighty has put into the hearts of His slaves.'" In one variant we find, "...which Allah has put into the hearts of those of His slaves He wills. Allah shows mercy to those of His slaves who are merciful."

There is no doubt that when there is mercy in the hearts of parents it is a help from Allah to assist them to bring up their children in a way that will please Allah and His Messenger. In the case of a father, mercy might even take the form of the apparent harshness he shows in order to spare his son the Blazing Fire of the Next World. Excessive love for a son, on the other hand, is one of the promptings of Shaytan which might well lead a father to spoil his son and accede to all his demands, thereby leading him to Hell. We seek refuge with Allah!

So the Wise Lawgiver takes a clear and resolute line towards sons. They are the ultimate blessing and bounty from Allah and they are a trust for which parents are responsible. They must care for them and bring them up as proper Muslims so that Muslim society will be based on firm foundations and not on fragile twigs corrupted by indulgence and excessive love, because of the fathers' blindness to the Path of Truth and Correctness.

It is necessary to follow the true Islamic method of bringing up children. It is a sound upbringing that is in harmony with the heavenly Message. It lays down clear lines and waymarks on the path of light and faith. It does not leave children foundering like lost ships amid the tumultuous waves of the appetites and desires of their fathers, being sometimes pampered excessively and sometimes neglected reprehensibly. Come, my brother, and embrace the overflowing favour of the All-Generous by adopting His wise method to set up the pillars on firm foundations.

The Islamic method of bringing up children

A man came to 'Umar ibn al-Khattab, may Allah be pleased with him, to complain to him about his son's disobedience. 'Umar summoned the boy and upbraided him for disobeying his father and neglecting his duties.

"Amir al-Mu'minin," said the man's son, "doesn't a son have any rights over his father?"

"Yes, he does," replied 'Umar.

"What are they, Amir al-Mu'minin?"

"That he chooses his mother carefully, gives him a good name, and teaches him the Book (i.e. the Qur'an)."

"Amir al-Mu'minin, my father did not do any of these things. My mother was a black woman who belonged to a Magian. He named me Ju'al (dung beetle) and did not teach me a single letter of the Qur'an."

'Umar turned to the man and said to him, "You come to me to complain about the disobedience of your son when you betrayed him before he ever betrayed you and were bad to him before he was ever bad to you!"

'Umar made the father responsible for his son's disobedience because he had neglected his upbringing and care in the light of the wise method of Allah and His upright *Shari'a*.

Children are a trust and a responsibility

The first thing to take into account when looking at the method Islam advocates for the correct upbringing of children is the attitude that parents have towards their children: how they understand the relationship that exists between themselves and their children.

'Abdullah ibn 'Amr, may Allah be pleased with him, said that the Messenger of Allah, may Allah bless him and grant him peace, said, "It is enough sin for a man that he ruin the one he feeds."

Al-Hasan, may Allah be pleased with him, said that the Prophet of Allah, may Allah bless him and grant him peace, said: "Allah will question every shepherd about what he tends, preserves or loses, and a man will be questioned about the people of his household."

Ibn 'Umar said, "I heard the Messenger of Allah, may Allah bless him and grant him peace, say, 'All of you are shepherds and each of you is responsible for his flock. An Imam is a shepherd and he is responsible for those in his care. A man is a shepherd in respect of his family and is responsible for those in his care. The woman is a shepherd in respect of her husband's house and is responsible for those in her care. The servant is a shepherd in respect of his master's property and is responsible for what is in his care. All of you are shepherds and each of you is responsible for his flock.'"

These *hadiths* define the general relationship of parents to their children. The Messenger of Allah also gave us detailed guidance and certain specific instructions within the broad framework of this responsibility so that the upbringing of children would not be left to the conflicting whims and desires of individual fathers.

Ibn 'Abbas said that the Prophet, may Allah bless him and grant him peace, said, "The first words you say to your children should be, 'There is no god but Allah.'" The Messenger, may Allah bless him and grant him peace, wanted the statement of *tawhid* to be the first thing a child hears, the first thing his tongue utters and the first phrase he understands.

The first thing a child should be made to understand is what is *halal* and what is *haram*. Ibn 'Abbas said, "Act in obedience to Allah and fear acts of disobedience to Allah. Instruct your children to obey Allah's commands and avoid what He has forbidden. That is a protection against the Fire for both you and them."

'Abdullah ibn 'Amr ibn al-'As, may Allah be pleased with him, said that the Messenger of Allah, may Allah bless him and grant him peace, said, "Order your children to pray when they are seven.

Beat them to make them do it when they are ten, and separate them in their beds." Analogous with the prayer is the practice of fasting certain days. Similarly the child should be taught to obey Allah and carry out His duties and be thankful to Him.

'Ali said that the Prophet, may Allah bless him and grant him peace, said, "Teach your children three qualities: love of your Prophet, love of the people of his family, and recitation of the Qur'an. Those who know the Qur'an will be in the shade of Allah's Throne on the Day when there is no shade except His shade together with His Prophets and pure ones."

A branch of their instruction should be the study of the life of the Messenger of Allah, may Allah bless him and grant him peace, and his expeditions with his noble Companions, and the study of the decisive battles of Islam.

Children should be taught trust and responsibility and sound belief and protected as far as possible from the godless propaganda of the people of disbelief, misguidance and doubt.

The legal obligation of children's maintenance

Abu Hurayra, may Allah be pleased with him, said that the Messenger of Allah, may Allah bless him and grant him peace said, "Out of a dinar you spend in the way of Allah and a dinar you spend to free a slave and a dinar you give to the poor and a dinar you spend on your family, the one with the greatest reward is the one you spend on your family."

Thawban, the client of the Messenger of Allah, said, "Is not the best dinar a man spends the dinar he spends on his family, the dinar he spends on his mount in the way of Allah, and the dinar he spends on his companions in the way of Allah?" Abu Qilaba said, "He began with the family." Then Abu Qilaba said, "Who could have a greater reward than someone who spends on young children and Allah increases them by him or Allah helps and enriches them?"

Abu Hurayra, may Allah be pleased with him, said that the Messenger of Allah, may Allah bless him and grant him peace, said, "I was shown the first three to enter the Garden and the first three to enter the Fire. The first three to enter the Garden will be a martyr, a slave who worshipped his Lord well and attended to the best interests of his master, and a chaste abstinent man with a family. The first three to enter the Fire will be an overbearing ruler, someone with property who did not pay the due of Allah on it, and a boastful poor person."

Sa'd ibn Abi Waqqas said that the Messenger of Allah, may Allah bless him and grant him peace, said to him, "You will be rewarded for everything you spend on your family, desiring by it the Face of Allah, even for the morsel you pop into your wife's mouth."

Ibn Mas'ud al-Badri related that the Prophet, may Allah bless him and grant him peace, said, "When a man spends out on behalf of his family and sincerely hopes to be rewarded for it, it counts as *sadaqa*."

Al-Miqdam ibn Ma'dikarib said that the Messenger of Allah, may Allah bless him and grant him peace, said, "What you give yourself to eat is *sadaqa* for you. What you give your children to eat is *sadaqa* for you. What you give your wife to eat is *sadaqa* for you. What you give your servant to eat is *sadaqa* for you."

'Abdullah ibn Mas'ud, may Allah be pleased with him, said that the Messenger of Allah, may Allah bless him and grant him peace, said, "The upper hand is better than the lower hand. Begin with your dependants: your mother, sister, brother, and so on."

Abu Hurayra, may Allah be pleased with him, related that one day the Messenger of Allah, may Allah bless him and grant him peace, said to his Companions, "Give *sadaqa*." A man said, "Messenger of Allah, I have a dinar." He said, "Spend it on yourself." He said, "I have another." He said, "Spend it on your wife." He said, "I have another." He said, "Spend it on your child." He said, "I have another." He said, "Spend it on your servant." He said, "I have another." He said, "Do what you see best with it."

Ka'b ibn 'Ujra said, "A man passed by the Prophet, may Allah bless him and grant him peace, and the Companions of the Messenger of Allah could see his firmness and vigour. They said, 'Messenger of Allah, if only this man were fighting in the Way of Allah!' The Messenger of Allah, may Allah bless him and grant him peace, said, 'If he goes out to strive on behalf of his young children, he is fighting in the Way of Allah. If he goes out to strive on behalf of his aged parents, he is fighting in the Way of Allah. If he goes out to strive against his lower self to make it abstemious, he is fighting in the Way of Allah. But if he goes out to fight in order to show off and boast, he is fighting in the Way of Shaytan."

Abu Hurayra related that the Messenger of Allah, may Allah bless him and grant him peace, said, "Provision comes from Allah according to the need of the one receiving it. Fortitude comes from Allah according to the size of the affliction."

Jabir related that the Prophet, may Allah bless him and grant him peace, said, "The first thing to be placed in someone's balance will be what he spends on his family."

Spending on one's children is an absolute obligation stipulated by the *Shari'a* and a Muslim is rewarded for it. This is to ensure that children are not deprived and exposed to penury. However it is clear that it is a duty which should be kept within limits so that extravagance and snobbery play no part and so that children are not corrupted by luxury and excessive pampering. All of us should keep within the guidelines that the Noble Qur'an has so clearly laid out for us:

"Eat and drink but do not be extravagant. He does not love the extravagant." (7:31)

"Those who, when they spend, are neither extravagant nor mean, but take a stand between the two." (25:67)

"Do not keep your hand chained to your neck but do not extend it to its full extent, lest you sit there blamed and destitute." (17:29)

"Do not squander what you have. Squanderers are brothers to the shaytans, and Shaytan is ever ungrateful to his Lord." (17:26-27)

At the same time, meanness exposes children to many causes of social decay which eat away at the pillars of Muslim society like woodworm. Therefore, my Muslim brother, you must spend money on your children without either meanness or extravagance because this course of action means well-being for you, your children and all Muslim society. Excessive affluence, on the other hand, brings about the destruction of nations and peoples as Allah warns us in His Noble Qur'an:

> *"When We desire to destroy a city, We send a command to the affluent in it and they become wantonly deviant in it and the Decree is realised against it and We annihilate it completely."* (17:16)

Similarly, the Prophet cautioned us saying, "By Allah, I do not fear poverty for you, but I fear that this world will be opened up to you as it was opened up to those before you and you will compete for it as they did and it will destroy you as it destroyed them."

Impartiality between children

The bias shown by certain parents can lead to favouring one child over all the others or favouring sons over daughters or favouring some children over others on account of certain spiritual or material characteristics. This usually results in dissension and enmity between siblings or causes psychological conflict in the rejected children and the spoiling of the favoured ones. Islam rejects this type of behaviour, renouncing it in the strongest possible terms, because Islam is the *deen* of truth, justice and equality, the *deen* of love between people, the *deen* of upright natural patterning: *"Allah's natural form on which He made mankind."* (30:29)

Islam enjoins a cohesive society in which there is no internecine fighting or disputes. It desires our souls to be at peace, assuaged by the springs of truth and social justice, so that they become lamps to illuminate the confused and oppressed. Each vessel satisfies according to what it contains. The true Muslim disseminates all the principles of good and raises the banner of noble principles which the whole of humanity is searching for in the midst of the turbulence of the worldly conflicts in which it lives.

Listen therefore, my brother Muslim, to those directives of the Prophet that show us how to achieve impartiality between our children so that we forge well-balanced souls which know how to carry out the rights of Allah, how to respect their parents, how to be sincere towards their Lord, and how to proceed on the path of their Prophet in a manner which will put their society right.

Ibn Hibban related that the Prophet, may Allah bless him and grant him peace, said, "Allah shows mercy to a father who helps his son to be respectful towards him."

At-Tabari and others said, "Be equitable between your children where gifts are concerned."

Al-Bukhari and Muslim related from an-Nu'man ibn Bashir that his father went to the Messenger of Allah, may Allah bless him and grant him peace, and said, "I have given this son of mine one of my slaves." The Messenger of Allah said, "Did you give each of your children the same?" He said, "No." The Messenger of Allah said, "Take back the gift." In one variant, "The Messenger of Allah, may Allah bless him and grant him peace, said, "Did you do this for all your children?" He said, "No." He said, "Fear Allah and be fair regarding your children." My father returned and took that *sadaqa* back." In another variant we find, "The Messenger of Allah, may Allah bless him and grant him peace, said, 'Bashir, do you have any other children?' He said, 'Yes, I do.' He said, 'Did you give all of them the same?' He said, 'No.' He said, 'Do not make me a witness, for I will not be a witness to an injustice.' Then he said 'Do you want them all be equally dutiful to you?' He said, 'Yes indeed.' He said, 'Then do not do this.'"

Anas related that a man was once with the Prophet, may Allah bless him and grant him peace, when a son of his came to him. He kissed him and sat him on his knee. A daughter came and he sat her down in front of him. The Messenger of Allah said, "Don't you treat them equally?"

Concern for daughters

Islam is particularly concerned with daughters in view of the misery they endured in the time before Islam came, about which Allah Almighty says:

"When any of them is given the good news of a daughter, his face darkens and he is furious. He hides away from people because of the evil of the good news he has been given. Should he keep it ignominiously or bury it in the earth? How evil is the judgement that they make!"

(16:58-59)

Islam removed these vestiges of the earlier time and called for absolute equality and complete justice. There is no distinction between male and female in respect of the merciful behaviour and paternal kindness due to them. Allah makes it clear that the distribution of male and female children is entirely a matter of His will:

"To Allah belongs the kingdom of the heavens and the earth. He creates whatever He wills. He gives females to anyone He wills. He gives males to anyone He wills. Or He pairs them together, male and female, and He makes anyone He wills barren. He is All-Knowing, All-Powerful." (42:49)

"Their Lord responds to them: 'I will not let the deeds of any doer among you go to waste, male or female - the one is as the other.'" (3:195)

Because of the vestiges of residual prejudice in favour of males over females, Islam assigned a special reward to those who are given girls and bring them up well and care for them in a manner which is pleasing to Allah and His Messenger. They are the mothers of the future and must be welcomed and prepared for their role to produce great men who are able to bear the torch of the Message and illuminate the earth with light and fill it with truth and justice.

Ibn 'Abbas said that the Messenger of Allah, may Allah bless him and grant him peace, said, "If someone has a daughter and does not bury her alive or demean her or prefer his sons to her, it is mandatory for Allah to admit him to the Garden."

Al-Muttalib ibn 'Abdullah al-Makhzumi reported, "I visited Umm Salama, the wife of the Prophet, may Allah bless him and grant him peace, and she said, 'My son, shall I tell you what I heard from the Messenger of Allah?' I replied, 'Yes please, mother.' She said, 'I heard the Messenger of Allah, may Allah bless him and grant him peace, say, "Anyone who spends on two daughters or two sisters or female relatives can expect a reward for what he spent on them...They will shield him from the Fire."'"

Jabir, may Allah be pleased with him, reported that the Messenger of Allah, may Allah bless him and grant him peace, said, "If someone has three daughters and provides for them, is merciful to them, and cares for them, the Garden is absolutely mandatory for him." He was asked, "Messenger of Allah, and what if there are only two of them?" Jabir also said, "Even if there are only two of them." He said that some people think that he was asked about raising one daughter and said it held even in the case of only one.

Abu Hurayra related that the Prophet, may Allah bless him and grant him peace, said, "If someone has three daughters and is steadfast in caring for them in good times and bad, Allah will admit him to the Garden because of his mercy to them." A man asked, "And two, Messenger of Allah?" He said, "And two." A man asked, "Messenger of Allah, what about one?" He said, "And one."

'A'isha, may Allah be pleased with her, said: "A woman came to me with her two daughters to beg and I had nothing but a date which I gave to her. She divided it between her two daughters, not eating any of it herself. Then she got up and left. The Prophet came in to us and I told him about this and he observed, 'Anyone who is tried in any way on account of his daughters will find them to be a shield for him from the Fire.'"

Anas, may Allah be pleased with him, related that the Prophet, may Allah bless him and grant him peace, said, "I and anyone who brings up two girls until they come of age will be like the two fingers of one hand on the Day of Rising." One variant has, "He and I will enter the Garden like these two," and he indicated his index finger and the adjoining finger.

Abu Sa'id al-Khudri said that the Messenger of Allah, may Allah bless him and grant him peace, said, "Anyone who has three daughters, three sisters, two daughters, or two sisters, and treats them well and fears Allah regarding them, will have the Garden."

You spoke the truth, O Messenger of Allah! May Allah repay you with the best reward that He has ever given a Prophet on account of his people and a Messenger on account of his community. You replaced ignorant unjust concepts with principles of justice and equality and made the Muslims who were illuminated by your guidance cheerfully welcome newborn girls, whereas previously they used to hide away because of the evil of the news of their birth. They began to put females in the position appropriate to them, seeking the pleasure of Allah and His Messenger. If it had not been for your esteemed *Shari'a*, nations would not have prided themselves in what they have achieved regarding the status of women. You are the source of every virtue and you are the light which fills the horizon and the freedom for which every person in chains heaves a sigh.

Encouragement to discipline children

Islam encourages laying down precise guidelines for children to regulate their life and define their personalities and inculcate in them sound belief. They are the seedbed and buttress of the Islamic community and a most precious treasure which must be closely guarded and preserved from every blemish, misleading thought or unsteadiness. If the young become lost in the ocean of life the whole community is lost with them and other nations fall on them as wolves fall on their prey. That is why we see the Messenger, may the blessings of Allah be upon him, stressing the importance of teaching children manners.

Jabir ibn Samura, may Allah be pleased with him, said that the Messenger of Allah, may Allah bless him and grant him peace, said, "It is a better for man to teach his son than to give away a *sa'* in *sadaqa*."

Ayyub ibn Musa said that the Messenger of Allah, may Allah bless him and grant him peace, said, "A parent cannot give his child a better gift than good manners."

Ibn Maja related from Ibn 'Abbas from the Prophet, may Allah bless him and grant him peace, "Honour children and give them good manners."

The Messenger, may Allah bless him and grant him peace, addressed fathers and urged them to teach their children manners since fathers have great influence over the course of the development, beliefs and personality of their children. The Prophet said, "Every child is born on the natural form and then his parents make him a Jew or a Christian or a Magian."

Other educational principles

We have already examined some of the principles which our beloved Prophet instructed fathers to follow in bringing up their children. We will now give some examples of his noble guidance for the education of children and familiarising them with praiseworthy conduct.

Parents should always be truthful so that they are a model for their children. 'Abdullah ibn 'Amir, may Allah be pleased with him, reported, "One day my mother called me while the Messenger of Allah, may Allah bless him and grant him peace, was sitting in our house. She said, "'Abdullah, come here and I will give you something.' He, peace and blessings upon him, asked, 'What are you going to give him?' She said, 'I am going to give him a date.' He said, 'If you did not give him anything, a lie would be written against you.'"

Truly the Prophet, may Allah bless him and grant him peace, was the living example of the virtues of the Qur'an, and the active embodiment of its eternal directives. He is the one who said about himself, "My Lord taught me manners and He taught me excellent manners." He is the good model, the guiding mercy and the light which illumines the lost and bewildered.

Parents should pursue a course of mercy with children so that it becomes their course of conduct in life. An-Nasa'i and al-Hakim related: "Once while the Messenger of Allah, may Allah bless him and grant him peace, was leading the people in prayer, al-Husayn came in. He climbed onto his shoulder while he was in prostration. He remained in prostration for such a long time that the people thought that something had happened. He said, 'My grandson used me as a mount and climbed on my back and I did not want to rush him until he finished."

We know from the *Isaba* that the Prophet, may Allah bless him and grant him peace, used to play with al-Hasan and al-Husayn, may Allah be pleased with them. He would walk on his hands and knees and they would hang onto him from the sides. He would crawl along with them, saying, "What an excellent camel you have and what excellent saddle-bags you are!"

Anas, may Allah be pleased with him, related that the Prophet, may Allah bless him and grant him peace, said, "I start the prayer intending to make it long and then I hear the crying of a child and shorten my prayer because I know what the mother feels on account of the crying."

It is related from Anas in the two *Sahih* volumes that the Prophet passed by some children and greeted them. He said, "The Messenger of Allah, may Allah bless him and grant him peace, was in the habit of doing that."

Choosing good friends for children

The Prophet, may Allah bless him and grant him peace, said, "A man will follow the *deen* of his close friend, so let each of you look to the one he takes as a close friend" (at-Tirmidhi). A child's friends should be godfearing and virtuous so that he will acquire praiseworthy qualities from them. Part of Ibn Sina's advice about raising children was: "At school a child should be with children who have good manners and pleasing habits because children inevitably are influenced by and copy their friends."

There is no doubt that teaching children and working with them from an early age by giving them a righteous environment is what gives the best results and sweetest fruits. Teaching them when they are older is much more difficult because their emotional habits have become fixed and their conduct is sealed.

Instruction benefits children when they are young
   but it does not benefit them later on.
When you prune branches, they become straight and strong.
   Do not be lax or you will make the wood unfruitful and weak.

Teaching children what is lawful and unlawful

Ibn 'Abbas said that the Messenger of Allah, may Allah bless
him and grant him peace said, "Order your children to obey
Allah's commands and avoid His prohibitions. That will shield
them from the Fire."

'Abdullah ibn 'Amr ibn al-'As said that the Messenger of
Allah, may Allah bless him and grant him peace, said, "Instruct
your children to pray when they are seven. Beat them to make
them do it when they are ten and separate them in their beds."

'Abdullah ibn 'Amr ibn al-'As also said that the Messenger of
Allah, may Allah bless him and grant him peace, said, "One of the
major wrong actions is for a man to abuse his parents." They said,
"O Messenger of Allah, is it possible for a man to abuse his parents?" He said, "Yes. He may curse another man's father who in
turn curses his father, and curse another man's mother and he in
turn curses his mother."

'Umar ibn Abi Salama said, "I was a child under the guardian-
ship of the Messenger of Allah, may Allah bless him and grant
him peace, and my hand would wander around in the dish. The
Messenger of Allah, may Allah bless him and grant him peace,
said to me, 'Boy, say the Name of Allah Almighty and eat with
your right hand and eat what is in front of you.'"

Let us read those comprehensive Qur'anic *ayats* which deal
with a father teaching his son and leading him to the path of belief:

"When Luqman said to his son, exhorting him, 'O my
dear son, do not make any others co-partners with Allah.
Associating others with Him is a terrible wrong.' We
instructed man concerning his parents - his mother bore
him in weakness upon weakness and his weaning was
within two years: 'Be thankful to Me and to your parents.

With Me is your journey's end. If they endeavour to make you make something else co-partner with Me about which you have no knowledge, do not obey them. Keep their company in this world correctly and courteously but follow the way of him who turns to Me. Then to Me is your return and I will inform you about whatever you were doing.' 'O my son! Even if something has only the weight of a mustard-seed and is inside a rock or anywhere in the heavens or the earth, Allah will bring it out. Allah is All-Penetrating, All-Aware. O my son! Establish the prayer and command the right and forbid the wrong and be steadfast in the face of all that happens to you. That truly shows firm resolve." (31:12-16)

This exemplifies the way of Islam regarding children's education. Children are a blessing from Allah and a trust which He has delegated to us. So we must not follow baseless whims regarding them and play with their lives and allow them to squander their time in fruitless pastimes when there are in fact defined divine laws and instructions delineating the path they should take and the goal they should have in front of them. They are the seedbeds of society. If a seedbed is good and the water which waters it is good and the nutrients which feed it are good, then the crop will also be good. The message of Islam will achieve its aims and its people become the best community to emerge among mankind.

The Prophets and their sons

The Prophets are the best model for those who desire Allah and His Messenger because they lived their lives for Allah and by Allah. They are the chosen of Allah's creation. They strove against the desires of the lower self and the appetites, and their hearts and intellects were filled with light by the remembrance of Allah and their souls yearned for the Heavenly Assembly. This world and its attractions and adornment were unimportant in their estimation and not worth a gnat's wing in their eyes.

Wealth and sons are the highest adornment of the life of this world, as the Almighty tells us. The Prophets of Allah and His noble Messengers turned from them as they turned from every other worldly adornment. They looked on them as a trust to be fulfilled. *"Right actions which endure are better with your Lord."*

There is the example of Sayyiduna Ibrahim whom Allah gave a son after he had lost hope of having one because of his extreme old age. Nevertheless, his love for that child did not distract him from carrying out the commands of Allah. He went out in submission and contentment to leave his own child in a dry desert where there was neither vegetation nor water. His overriding preoccupation and supplication was that his Lord would make him and his descendants people who would establish the prayer.

The prayer is the foundation of the *deen* and it is the most important thing in life. It is life itself because it is the connection between the slave and his Lord. So what about when this slave is the Friend of Allah and the Father of the Prophets, Ibrahim? He must have known the pleasure of intimate conversation, the fervour of arrival, and total absorption in the prayer. He loved that above all other things and he was keen to establish his descendants in it. He left his son in a place which lacked even the basic necessities of life. There was no house, shelter or food. But the first thing he sought for them was the food of the spirit, which is the prayer, and only after that food for the body, which is the fruit of this world.

Listen to those Qur'anic *ayats* which tell us of this thereby showing to us the greatest possible example of striving against the lower self: a father, who was a Prophet, carrying out the teachings of his Lord, unaffected by his attachment to his only son for whom he had yearned for his entire life. The Almighty says in His Noble Book:

> *"Our Lord, I have settled some of my offspring in a valley where there is no cultivation near to Your Sacred House. Our Lord, may they establish the prayer! Make the hearts of mankind incline towards them and provide them with fruits, so that perhaps they will be thankful. Our Lord, You know what we keep hidden and what we make public. Nothing is hidden from Allah either in the earth or*

72

in heaven. Praise be to Allah Who has given me, despite my old age, Isma'il and Ishaq. My Lord is the Hearer of prayer. My Lord, make me and my descendants people who establish the prayer. My Lord, accept this supplication." (14:37-40)

This was the trial of our Master Ibrahim before which all other trials pale into insignificance and besides which all other difficulties seem small. Allah wanted the heart of our Master Ibrahim to be sincerely devoted to Him without the slightest grain of love for his son or anything else in it. He wanted to give an example to the believers that would make them submit in love of Allah and pursue His pleasure and carry out His commands even if doing that entailed the sacrifice of "an intelligent lad" who filled the heart and eye with love because of his youth, tender nature and belief in Allah:

> *"When he was of an age to work with him, he said, 'My son, I saw in a dream that I was sacrificing you, so look to what you think.' He said, 'O father, do as you are ordered to. You will find me, Allah willing, one of the steadfast.' Then when they had both submitted and he had thrown him face-down on the ground, We called out to him, 'O Ibrahim! You have confirmed the vision. This is the way We recompense good-doers.' This most certainly was the ultimate trial. And We redeemed him with a mighty sacrifice and left the later people saying of him: 'Peace be upon Ibrahim.' That is the way We recompense good-doers. He truly was one of Our believing slaves."* (37:102-111)

The Prophets of Allah carry out the command of Allah, even if that obliges them to sacrifice their own sons. We learn from this that nothing is higher than love of our sons except love of Allah. We can also see this clearly manifest in the story of our Master Nuh. When the flood came Allah ordered him to take the believers with him in the Ark which he had made. Out of his compassion as a father he called out to his son to travel the path of belief with him and not to remain with the unbelievers. But his son refused and persisted in his obduracy until he became one of those who were drowned. When Nuh implored his Lord to give him his misguided obdurate son, Allah informed him that doing that was not a righteous action and that belief and disbelief in Allah and the Path of Allah had distinguished between them. Then Nuh sought his Lord's forgiveness and asked Him to forgive him and show mercy to him for asking for something about which he had no knowledge. He cast paternal compassion behind him because the message of truth, good and light is more important than misplaced compassion. The Almighty tells us what happened between Nuh and his son in His Noble Book:

"Until when Our command came, and the oven boiled over, We said, 'Load into it a pair of every kind, and your family - except for him against whom word has already gone ahead - and all who believe.' But those who believed with him were only a few. He said, 'Embark in it. In the name of Allah be its voyage and its landing! Assuredly my Lord is Forgiving, Merciful.' It ran with them amid waves like mountains, and Nuh called out to his son, who had kept himself apart, 'My son! Come on board with us. Do not be with the unbelievers!' He said, 'I will go to a mountain for refuge. It will protect me from the water.' He said, 'There is no protector today from Allah's command except for him on whom He has mercy.' And the waves came between them and he was one of the drowned. It was said, 'O Earth, swallow up your water!' and, 'O Heaven, hold back your rain!' And the water subsided and the affair was concluded and the Ark came to land on al-Judi. And it was said, 'Good riddance to the people of the wrongdoers!' Nuh called out to his Lord and said, 'My Lord, my son is one of my family and Your promise is surely the Truth and You are the justest of judges.' He said, 'Nuh, he is definitely not of your family. He is one whose action is other than righteous. Do not, therefore, ask Me for something about which you do not have knowledge. I

admonish you lest you become one of the ignorant.' He said, 'My Lord, I seek refuge with You from asking You for something about which I have no knowledge. If You do not forgive me and have mercy on me, I will certainly be one of the lost.'" (11:40-47)

Our Master Ya'qub travelled the path of the Prophets whose goal is the sublime Essence of Allah and he directed his sons accordingly. He took the hand of the one in whose spirit he sensed true aspiration and directed him in his spiritual development and was steadfast in the face of the behaviour of the thoughtless among his sons who were misguided from path, in the hope that Allah would guide them by His bounty and mercy. He was a Prophet who had to carry out what he was commanded to do, able to remind but not able to compel. Allah guides whomever He will. His sons were in fact part of the message he brought, showing us how humanity can be liberated from the shackles of untamed human nature to the sublimity of true submission to Allah.

His son Yusuf came to him and told him about a dream he had had and, by the light of prophethood, Our Master Ya'qub was aware that the dream was true and that his son had an exalted destiny. So he gave him sound advice not to recount the dream to his brothers and to be on guard against Shaytan because he is a clear enemy to man. He told him to strive to gain the pleasure of Allah so that His Lord chose him, taught him and completed His blessing upon him as He had done before in the case of Ibrahim and his descendants:

"When Yusuf told his father, 'Father! I saw eleven bright stars, and the sun and moon as well. I saw them all prostrate in front of me.' He said, 'My dear son, do not tell your brothers your dream lest they devise some ploy to injure you. Shaytan is a clear-cut enemy to man. Accordingly your Lord will pick you out and teach you the interpretation of events and perfectly fulfil His blessing on you, as well as on the family of Ya'qub, as He fulfilled it per-

fectly before upon your forebears, Ibrahim and Ishaq.
Most certainly your Lord is Knowing, Wise.'" (12:4-6)

With the help of his prophetic insight and fortitude Ya'qub was able to understand and accept the thoughtless impetuosity of his other sons:

> *"It is merely that your lower selves have recommended something, which you did. But steadfast patience, that is beautiful. It is Allah alone who is my Help in face of the event that you portray."* (12:18)
>
> *"He said, 'It is merely that your lower selves have recommended something, which you did. But steadfast patience, that is beautiful. Perhaps Allah will bring them all together. He is indeed the Knowing and the Wise.'"*
> (12:83)

This Prophet who was also a father strove in his life as his Lord had commanded and suffered the loss of the two things to which the souls of mankind are most attached, his beloved son Yusuf and later his eyesight. What, however, was his preoccupation at the time of his death? Did he weep over parting from his family? Did he talk to them of their livelihood and inheritance? Did he merely enjoy the family gathering? No, his overriding preoccupation was to make sure that the basic elements of the *deen* were strong and in place. That is the task of the Prophets even in their darkest moments. The Message must be conveyed and the trust carried out even when the Prophet is struggling in the throes of death:

> *"Ibrahim directed his sons to this, as did Ya'qub: 'My sons! Allah has chosen this deen for you, so do not die except as Muslims who submit.' Or were you present when death came to Ya'qub and he said to his sons, 'What will you worship after me?' They said, 'We will worship your God, the God of your fathers, Ibrahim and Isma'il and Ishaq - One God. We are Muslims submitted to Him.'"*
> (2:132-133)

76

May the peace of Allah be upon His Prophets who strove in His way and lighted the way for us so that we might be illuminated by their guidance and strive against our lower selves and direct our steps towards establishing the principles of truth and future generations of Muslims with sound belief on the Straight Path.

O Allah, guide us by Your guidance and keep us from the trials of life and death! Purify our hearts of lower appetites and fill them with the light of the Noble Qur'an! We ask you by the supplication of the devout Prophet Da'ud who used to pray to You in these words:

"O Allah! I ask You for four things and I seek refuge with You from four things. I ask You for a remembering tongue, for a thankful heart, for a body capable of enduring affliction, and for a wife who will help me in both my *deen* and this world. I seek refuge with You from property which is bad for me, from a child who becomes my master, from a neighbour who fails to acknowledge any good he has from me and who discloses any evil he sees from me, and from a wife who makes me go prematurely grey!"

As for our Master Muhammad, may Allah bless him and grant him peace, he was the noblest of creation, the Master of the Messengers and the best of teachers. Nothing distracted him from Allah and he is the highest example for us. He is the one who called on Allah with the words: "O Allah! Make the food of the family of Muhammad what is just sufficient for their needs!" He did not want this world for them as Allah did not want it for them. Preoccupation with food and drink puts one far from the pleasure of Allah and spiritual growth.

He is the one who said: "The house of prophethood should be the first to go hungry when the people go hungry and the last to be filled when the people are filled."

He is the one who refused to give his daughter a servant despite the hardness of her life and advised her to seek help by remembering Allah and dividing the work between herself and her husband 'Ali, may Allah be pleased with him.

77

He is the one who woke up the people of his house for the *Fajr* prayer and said to them, *"Allah desires to remove all impurity from you, o People of the House, and to purify you completely."* (33:33)

He is the one who insisted on establishing the *hadd* punishments of Allah and was angry when Usama ibn Zayd interceded for someone when one of the *hudud* of Allah was broken. He said, may the blessings of Allah be on him, "Even if Fatima, the daughter of Muhammad, had stolen, I would have cut off her hand."

This is the limit of sublimity in love of Allah. Children are not the goal. They are a trust and a means to please Allah. However great his love for his daughter Fatima was, this love would not have made him hesitate to implement the command of Allah and preserve His limits. How could that not be, when he is the greatest teacher of mankind? He said: "Carrying out one of the *hudud* of Allah is better than forty days of rain in the land of Allah." Ibn Maja related this from Ibn 'Umar.

He said, "None of you will believe until I am dearer to him than his wealth, his child and all people." Al-Bukhari and Muslim related it.

This is what is desired from the Muslim: his belief is not complete until the love of the Messenger and his *Shari'a* is put before love of wealth, children and all people. The Messenger is the one whose character was the Qur'an and who was taught correct behaviour by His Lord. Love of Allah, the *Shari'a* and carrying out the Message for which Allah had made him responsible was dearer to him than the entire world and all it contains. At the beginning of his mission he spoke to his uncle with words which demonstrate absolute certainty, resolve and love of Allah: "By Allah, uncle," he said, "if they were to put the sun in my right hand and the moon in my left hand on condition that I abandoned this mission, I would not do so until Allah vindicates it or I die in the process."

May Allah bless you and grant you peace,
O Signpost of guidance!
You are the lamp of every virtue.
All lights issue from your light.

Every virtue in the universe is from the virtue of the Prophet
which the excellent can only borrow.

Your words, O Messenger of Allah, are words regarding the
incomparable *Shari'a* which is more exalted than heaven itself.
How can we attain to it, when it is something in search of which
necks crane upwards and which eyes are dazzled by looking at?
All we can do is ask Allah to give us success in following your
radiant *Shari'a*. That is the Great Victory and in it lies rescue from
every grief.

Islam's method for treating excessive love of children

Islam takes the clearest possible position towards excessive
love of children. Children are like any other of Allah's blessings.
There are two sides to them. On the one hand we have the right to
enjoy them but on the other we must show gratitude for them to
Allah Almighty. Blessings are one of the means of consolidating
man in the life of this world, but the goal is worship of Allah alone
- glory be to Him and may He be exalted! - and carrying out the
duties owed to Him and striving to please Him by following His
commands and avoiding His prohibitions and following His
Straight Path to the best of our ability.

If we make the means the end, this will be making something
else co-partner with Allah: the heart not being sincere for Him
alone. This is the greatest calamity and a dangerous chute down
which it is all too easy for a man to slip. It is what the Messenger,
may Allah bless him and grant him peace, described as a concealed trap.

That is why the teachings of the Qur'an are so stern regarding
people who love their sons more than striving in the way of Allah
and His pleasure and raising the banner of Allah high. The
Almighty says in His Noble Book:

> *"Say: 'If your fathers or your sons or your brothers or
> your wives or your tribe, or any wealth you have acquired,*

or any business you fear may decline, or places to live which please you, are dearer to you than Allah and His Messenger and jihad in His way, then wait until Allah brings about His command. Allah does not guide the wantonly deviant.'" (9:24)

"You will not find a people who believe in Allah and the Last Day having love for anyone who opposes Allah and His Messenger, though they be their fathers or their sons or their brothers or their clan. Those people, Allah has inscribed belief within their hearts and will reinforce them with a Spirit from Him and admit them into Gardens with rivers flowing under them, in them timelessly, forever. Allah is pleased with them and they are pleased with Him. Those are the party of Allah. Certainly it is the party of Allah who are successful." (58:22)

"As for those who reject, their wealth and children will not avail them against Allah in any way. They are the fuel of the Fire." (3:10)

"It is not your wealth or your children that will bring you close in nearness to Us, except in the case of those who believe and act rightly. Those ones shall have a double recompense for what they did. They will be safe from all harm in the highest part of Paradise." (34:37)

"O you who believe! Do not allow your wealth or your children to divert you from the remembrance of Allah. Any who do that are the losers." (63:9)

"Your relatives and your children will not benefit you on the Day of Rising. He will distinguish between you. Allah sees everything you do." (60:3)

"O you who believe! In your wives and your children there is an enemy for you so beware of them. And if you pardon and overlook and forgive, Allah is All-Forgiving, All-Merciful. Your wealth and children are only a trial. But there is an immense reward with Allah."

(64:14-15)

"Know that your wealth and your children are a trial, and that there is an immense reward with Allah." (8:28)

"Do not marvel at their wealth and their children. Allah merely desires to punish such people by them during their lives in this world, and for their souls to depart while they are still rejectors." (9:55)

"Neither their wealth nor their children will avail them in any way against Allah. Those are the Companions of the Fire. They shall be in it timelessly, forever." (58:17)

"O Mankind! Fear your Lord, and fear a Day when no father will be able to compensate for his son, and no son able to compensate for his father, in any way. Allah's promise is true. Do not therefore let the life of this world delude you; and do not let the Deluder delude you concerning Allah." (31:33)

See how the *ayats* repeatedly make the situation clear and call on us to remember constantly that wealth, children, wives, family and relatives and everyone and everything on the earth are evanescent and simply the touchstone for telling the degree of the believer's belief in his Lord and how he follows His path. So the true believer who is pleased with Allah as his Lord, Islam as his *deen*, and Muhammad, may Allah bless him and grant him peace, as his Messenger should not become preoccupied with the substance of his test. He should not enjoy it in a manner which will hinder him from carrying out the trust he bears from Allah so that he becomes ignorant and unjust.

Children will not be of any help to their parents on the Day of Judgement except in respect of the efforts and sacrifices which parents have made on their behalf in the way of Allah and His Messenger. Parents should be on their guard against the temptation to love their children overmuch because such love makes people blind and deaf to the truth and so becomes a stumbling block to the perfection of a person's faith, as the Beloved of the Truth and Master of creation, may the blessings and peace of Allah be upon him, informed us:

81

Al-Bukhari related from Anas, may Allah be pleased with him, that the Messenger of Allah, may Allah bless him and grant him peace, said, "Whoever possesses three attributes will experience the sweetness of faith: that he loves Allah and His Messenger more than anything else, that he loves someone for the sake of Allah alone, and that he hates the prospect of reverting to disbelief as much as he would hate being thrown into the Fire."

Al-Bukhari also related that 'Umar ibn al-Khattab, may Allah be pleased with him, said to the Prophet, may Allah bless him and grant him peace, "Messenger of Allah, you are dearer to me than anything except my self which is between my sides." The Prophet said, "None of you will believe until I am dearer to him than his own self." 'Umar said, "By the One who sent down the Book on you, you are dearer to me than my self which is between my sides." The Prophet said to him, "Now, 'Umar, now your belief is complete."

It is confirmed in the *Sahih* that the Messenger of Allah, may Allah bless him and grant him peace, said, "None of you will truly believe until his desires are in line with what I have brought."

Al-Bukhari and Muslim related that the Messenger of Allah, may Allah bless him and grant him peace, said, "None of you will believe until he loves me more than his property, his children and all people."

✸✶✸✶✸

Truly Allah has made love of children instinctive to man so that it may enable him to endure all the hardship and effort he encounters in bringing his children up and help him to carry out his responsibility towards them. But Allah - glory be to Him and may He be exalted! - desires that that instinct be balanced and in measure so that there is neither excess nor negligence, either of which might expose children to being lost in the sea of life. Islam needs bright new generations who can take on the burden of the Message. It needs lofty spirits who yearn for the Heavenly Assembly, seek Divine Love and taste the pleasure of the connection between earth and heaven. This can only be achieved through love of Allah and His Messenger, a love which firstly fills the heart and is then given form by following the path which Allah has outlined in His Immense Qur'an.

The Beloved Messenger demonstrated this path in his *Sunna* in word and deed. The Messenger, may Allah bless him and grant him peace, is a mercy for us in this world and the Next and his guidance keeps us from the harmful effects of our appetites and protects us from the fires of this world and the Next. As one of the righteous said, "In respect of the appetites of this world, man is like a moth which tries to fly into the flame. When the fires of the appetites appear to man and he fails to realise the lethal poison which lies within them, he continues to fling himself at them until he becomes enveloped by them, bound by them, and is completely and utterly destroyed. If only human beings had the innocence of moths! When a moth is deceived by the outward flame, it is burned up and vanishes away. But man will remain in the Fire forever and ever.

That is why the Messenger of Allah, may Allah bless him and grant him peace, used to call and say, "I hold you back from the Fire by your belts while you are hurtling towards it like moths."

O Allah! Give us success in following Your beloved Prophet so that we emerge from the bondage of our selves and appetites into the vast freedom of Your pleasure. Give us success in doing what pleases You. You are the best Master and the best Helper. We seek the help of none but You and we seek assistance from none but You. We direct our eyes towards You and fill our hearts with Your Greatness and Power. Make our hearts and spirits attentive to that holy *hadith* which You revealed to Sayyiduna Da'ud, the penitent slave, when You said to him:

"O Da'ud, by My Might and Majesty, none of My slaves seeks My help rather than that of My creation when I know that to be his intention, even if the seven heavens and everyone in them and the seven earths and everyone in them are conspiring against him, without my appointing for him an escape and an opening. By My Might and Majesty and Immensity, none of My slaves seeks protection from any creature instead of Me when I know that to be his intention without the connection between him and heaven being cut and the earth giving way beneath him. I do not care in which valley he is destroyed."

Truly the nobility and distinction of the slave consist of his contemplating his Almighty Lord, responding to Him, relying on Him and depending on Him. His baseness and falling in Allah's esteem come from his looking at himself, turning to other than Allah and relying on other than Allah. O Allah! Do not place us among those who are distracted by their wealth and children from remembering You! Let our hearts be with You and our aspiration be for you! Help us in remembering You, being thankful to You, worshipping You well, and carrying out Your message in the way which pleases You best, O Lord! Your pleasure is better than this world and everything it contains.

Chapter Four
The Islamic Remedy for Excessive Love of Wealth

It would be a good idea, at this point, to remind ourselves of the noble *ayat* which was mentioned at the beginning of our definition of the appetites:

> *"For mankind the love of worldly appetites is painted in glowing colours: women and children, heaped-up mounds of gold and silver, horses with distinctive markings, livestock, and fertile farmland. All that is merely the enjoyment of the life of this world. But the best homecoming is into the Presence of Allah."* (3:14)

We find here that there are six general categories of appetites which the Almighty mentions in His Noble Book, two of which are connected to women and children, and four of which are connected to wealth, whether in the form of money or goods. This is what has led us to put them under a single heading, because Allah - glory be to Him and may He be exalted! - says:

> *"Wealth and sons are the embellishment of the life of this world. Right actions which remain are better with your Lord in respect of reward and better with regard to hope."* (18:46)

Wealth, whether in money or goods, has a alluring aspect which absorbs both heart and mind. That is why Allah only mentions wealth in the Qur'an as something transient and why He says, *"Right actions which remain are better with your Lord."* Sometimes He mentions it as a temptation in the path of the believer put there to test the strength of his belief, at others as an enemy which distracts man from remembering Allah and leads him to the depths of the Fire from which there is no escape and where regret will be of no avail. At its best wealth is a trust for the believer which he must use in the manner that has been delineated for him by Allah in the *Shari'a* of Islam: for *zakat,* as *sadaqa,* to promote solidarity between the Muslims, for festivals and weddings, to help alleviate the distress of misfortunes and disasters. Even the daily expenditure of a Muslim is subject to what Allah has ordained in His Noble Book:

> *"Those who, when they spend, are neither extravagant nor mean, but take a stand between the two."* (25:67)

Without a doubt, wealth is the mainstay of life and an immense trust. We are commanded to spend it immediately after being commanded to believe in Allah and His Messenger:

> *"Believe in Allah and His Messenger and spend from that to which He has made you successors. Those of you who do believe and spend out will have an immense reward."* (57:7)

Every expense, large or small, is known to Allah:

> *"Whatever amount you spend or vow you make, Allah knows it. The wrongdoers have no helpers."* (2:270)
>
> *"Nor do they spend any amount, large or small, nor do they cut across any valley, without it being written for them, so that Allah can repay them for the best of what they were doing."* (9:121)

Owing to the immense importance of wealth and because of its potential both for good and evil, the *Shari'a* of Allah deals with it in depth and shows us how to strike a balance between instinctive covetousness and wasteful extravagance. Balance is a principle which lies at the very heart of existence:

> *"He erected heaven and established the balance, so that you would not overstep in the balance. Give just weight, therefore; do not skimp in the balance."* (55:7-9)

In view of the intensity of the appetite of love of wealth and in order to balance the two sides of the scale, Islam has laid down a rigorous set of laws regulating the circulation of wealth in Muslim society and to keep the desire for wealth in check. If it had been left uncurbed, society would have been destroyed by the ferocity of unrestrained human voracity.

These laws which the All-Wise Lawgiver has laid down include being moderate in seeking and acquiring wealth, being cautious about love of wealth and desire for it, the necessity of acquiring wealth only from lawful sources, the prohibition of usury, the prohibition of hoarding, the prohibition of cheating, the prohibition of tampering with weights and measures, the prohibition of theft and misappropriation, the regulation of debts, and the obligation of *zakat* and *sadaqa* as the basis of the circulation of surplus wealth in Muslim society.

With the will and help of Allah, we will deal with these points in detail one by one in order to demonstrate the immense wisdom of our Creator in basing our societies on firm foundations of truth, justice and security and the greatness of His Messenger in conveying the Message and carrying out the trust. The details of what the Noble Qur'an sets down remain applicable no matter what changes take place in the human situation and will, if properly applied, achieve the progress desired for society. Let us, therefore, devote some time to learning these things which contain such good, salvation and success for all of us by the aid and help of Allah.

The principles of the Islamic remedy for excessive love of wealth

Moderation in seeking and acquiring wealth

The Prophet, may the blessings and peace of His Lord be upon him, said, "Wealth is verdant and sweet. It is an excellent companion for the Muslim who gives some of it to the poor, the orphan and the traveller. But if he takes it without having any right to it, he is like someone who eats and does not become full and it will be a witness against him on the Day of Rising."

Wealth is verdant and sweet because it is the mainstay of life and the basis of civilisation, society and people's comfort. It is an excellent companion and helper for the Muslim as long as he gives those who have a right to it their due and protects the divinely stipulated rights of others. This applies on condition that it is not obtained through robbery or usurpation but only by such lawful means as are defined by the rules of belief based on nobility, chastity and trustworthiness. The wealth which enters our pockets as money and of which we spend will be a witness against us on the Day of Rising and consequently will play a part in deciding our ultimate destination in the Next World in addition to the part it plays in our lives in this world.

My brother Muslim, there is a whole body of noble Prophetic *hadiths* dealing with the issue of wealth, not in the statistical way used by economists and sociologists but rather with the wisdom of the Messenger and the insight of the teacher. It does not connect the problems of wealth and property to market forces and the currents of history but rather to the stirrings of conscience, the fountains of the spirit and the pure *Shari‘a* of Allah.

Jabir, may Allah be pleased with him, related that the Messenger of Allah, may Allah bless him and grant him peace, said, "Do not consider your provision slow in arriving. No self will die until it has received its provision in full. Be moderate in asking. Take what is lawful and leave what is unlawful."

It is related that al-Hasan, may Allah be pleased with him, said, "The Messenger of Allah, may Allah bless him and grant him peace, climbed the *minbar* on the day of the expedition to Tabuk. He praised Allah and then said, "O people! I only command you as Allah commands you and I only forbid you what Allah forbids you. Be moderate in asking. By the One who has the soul of Abu'l-Qasim in His hand, one of you seeking his provision is like someone seeking his term. If any of it is difficult for you, seek it with obedience to Allah Almighty.'"

Abu Dharr, may Allah be pleased with him, said, "The Messenger of Allah. may Allah bless him and grant him peace, began to recite this *ayat: 'If anyone fears Allah, He will give him a way out and provide for him from somewhere he does not expect'* (65:2-3). He repeated it again and again to the point that I dozed off. He said, 'O Abu Dharr, if even the most sinful of people were to hold to this, it would be enough for him."

Abu'd-Darda', may Allah be pleased with him, said that the Messenger of Allah, may Allah bless him and grant him peace, said, "The sun never rises without two angels being sent with it who call out and are heard by all the inhabitants of the earth except for men and jinn: 'O people! Come to your Lord. What is little and sufficient is better than what is abundant but distracting.' The sun never sets without two angels being sent with it who call out and are heard by all the inhabitants of the earth except for men and jinn: 'O Allah! Reimburse him who spends and destroy him who withholds.'"

Anas, may Allah be pleased with him, said that the Messenger of Allah, may Allah bless him and grant him peace, said, "If this world is the goal and hope of anyone and he is fixed on it and wants it, Allah will make poverty his lot and disorder his affairs and only what is written for him will come to him. If the Next World is the goal and hope of anyone and he is fixed on it and wants it, Allah will place sufficiency in his heart and order his affairs and this world will come to him submissively."

It is related that Ibn 'Abbas said, "The Messenger of Allah, may Allah bless him and grant him peace, addressed us in the mosque of al-Khayf and praised Allah and mentioned Him as He deserves. Then he said, 'If this world is a person's aspiration, Allah will disorder his affairs and make poverty his lot and only give him what is written for him.'"

Anas, may Allah be pleased with him, related that the Messenger of Allah, may Allah bless him and grant him peace, said, "Four things are aspects of ultimate wretchedness: dullness of the eye, hardness of the heart, excessive expectations, and desire for this world."

'Abdullah ibn Mas'ud, may Allah be pleased with him, said, "Do not show approval of anyone at the expense of the wrath of Allah. Do not praise anyone for the bounty Allah has given him. Do not blame anyone for what Allah has not given him. The provision of Allah will not be driven towards you by the desire of any desirer nor turned from you by the dislike of any disliker. In His fairness and justice, Allah has placed rest and release in His pleasure and certainty and worry and sorrow in His wrath."

Ka'b ibn Malik, may Allah be pleased with him, said that the Messenger of Allah, may Allah bless him and grant him peace, said, "Two hungry wolves loose among sheep do not cause as much damage as is caused to a man's *deen* by his greed for money and reputation."

Abu Hurayra, may Allah be pleased with him, related that the Messenger of Allah, may Allah bless him and grant him peace, used to say, "O Allah! I seek refuge with You from knowledge which does not benefit, a heart which is not humble, a self which is not satisfied, and a supplication which is not heard."

Anas, may Allah be pleased with him, said that the Messenger of Allah, may Allah bless him and grant him peace, said, "If the son of Adam were to have a valley full of gold, he would want two valleys, but his mouth will only be filled with dust. Allah turns to whoever turns in repentance."

The Prophet, the greatest mentor and guide of humanity to the Straight Path, may Allah bless him and grant him peace, knew without a doubt how great an enticement wealth is and how untameable man's appetites are. He perceived the hastiness and desperate struggles which the exigencies of daily life and the force of rivalry involve people in. He particularly addresses those who are wealthy, reminding them that Allah has given them their wealth as a trust and calling them to follow the *Shari'a* of Allah in their sorties into the world of acquisition and earning. This is elaborated in the Noble Qur'an:

> *"It is He who made the earth subservient to you, so walk its trails and eat of its provision. The Resurrection is to Him."* (67:15)

> *"O you who believe! When the prayer is called on the Day of Jumu'a, hurry to the remembrance of Allah and leave off trade. That is better for you if you did but know."* (62:9)

Walking, moderation, and good deportment are what should be displayed in the life of this world. Running, yearning and impatience should only be displayed in connection with the remembrance of Allah and desire for the Next World. It is only eternal bliss which merits extreme effort. The passing life of this world does not merit yearning and struggle because all provision is in the hands of Allah, the Provider. Provision comes from the Unseen and Allah gives it according to His knowledge and makes it descend by His decree. If He willed He could give it in abundance to people, for His treasures never end. But He limited it in order to test and try those who believe in the Unseen and rely on their Lord and are not moved by the slow arrival of provision to seek wealth from unlawful sources. The Prophet said, "Do not admire vainglorious fighting or people who amass unlawful wealth. If they give it away as *sadaqa*, it is not accepted from them, and what they do not give is simply their provision on their journey to the Fire."

The Messenger replied to those who are not satisfied and measure wealth by the criteria of possessions by saying to them, "Wealth does not lie in having a lot of goods. Wealth lies in the independence of the self." So wealth does not come from affluence and luxuries. Wealth is a matter of contentment, certainty and the blessing of Allah. All economists agree that the two major factors in any economic problem are expenditure and revenue and that the solution is reached either by reducing expenditure or increasing revenue. In view of the difficulty of increasing revenue, even at a national level, cutting expenditure is generally the best solution. When someone who cuts expenditure also yearns for needs which are higher - spiritual needs - then this solution is an even better one.

The contentment which Islam enjoins on us is the most precious of this world's treasures, because our noble Messenger informed us, "If any of you wakes up in the morning safe, healthy, and with enough food for that day, it is as if he possessed the entire world." We know that covetousness for the wealth of others can sweep us away. The Prophet, may Allah bless him and grant him peace, instructed us, "If any of you looks at someone who has been has been given greater wealth and provision than him, he should then look at someone who has less than him. That makes it more likely that he will not make light of the blessings Allah has given him. How can we make light of Allah's blessing when the Almighty says: *"Your Lord does not wrong the slaves"* (41:46)?

There are all sorts of blessings which many wealthy people are always trying to obtain but are unable to despite all their wealth. The provision of Allah is vast and varied. Lack of material things does not indicate a low position in the sight of Allah. It may on the contrary be the sign of His special spiritual gift, the hearts of whose recipients are filled with wealth and good. This is what our beloved Messenger, may Allah bless him and grant him peace, taught us when he said, "Allah gives this world to those He loves and those He does not love. He only gives the Next World to those He loves."

My Muslim brother, have confidence in the gift, bounty and generosity of Allah. Provision is in His hand alone and He is unstinting in His generosity and bounteousness. Do not let delays in the arrival of provision move you to leave the path of truth, even in thought. Constantly reflect on these clear *ayats* which should fill your heart with the certainty that Your provision is in the Hand of Allah and that He has appointed a specified term for everything.

"Your provision is in heaven - and what you are promised. By the Lord of heaven and earth, it is most certainly the truth, just as you have speech." (51:22-23)

"Allah increases provision for anyone He wills and restricts it." (13:26)

"I did not create jinn or man except to worship Me. I do not desire any provision from them. I do not desire for them to nourish Me. Truly Allah is the Provider, the Possessor of Strength, the Sure." (51:56-58)

"Say: 'Who gives you provision out of heaven and earth? Who has command over hearing and sight? Who extracts the living from the dead and extracts the dead from the living? Who directs the affair?' They will say, 'Allah.' So say, 'Will you not then be godfearing?'" (10:31)

"Rather He who originates creation and then will bring it back again and who provides for you from heaven and earth ... Is there a god besides Allah? Say: 'Produce your proof if you are telling the truth.' Say: 'None of those in the heavens and the earth knows the Unseen except Allah.'" (27:64-65)

"Who is it that is going to provide for you if He holds back His provision? Yet still they obstinately persist in insolence and shying away." (67:21)

"How many a creature does not carry its provision with it! Allah provides both for it and for you. He is the All-Hearing, the All-Knowing." (29:60)

"If anyone fears Allah, He will give him a way out and provide for him from somewhere he does not expect." (65:2-3)

"O mankind! Remember Allah's blessing to you. Is there any creator other than Allah providing for you from heaven and the earth? There is no god but Him. How then have you been perverted?" (35:3)

"If only the people of the cities had believed and been godfearing, We would have opened up to them blessings from heaven and earth." (7:96)

"If Allah were to give abundant provision to His slaves, they would act as tyrants on the earth. However He sends down what He wills in a measured way. He is aware of and He sees His slaves." (42:27)

This, my Muslim brother, is but a small selection of the clear miraculous *ayats* of Allah to put your heart to rest concerning the most pressing question to preoccupy the mind of any man on the face of the earth: the question of provision. Allah made it one of those unseen matters which contain many wisdoms, some of which we can see and others of which are veiled from us as a mercy to us because they are beyond the capacity of our intellects to bear. That is so that the believer may live in tranquillity and not exult in what comes to him nor grieve over what passes him by.

Provision is a determined quantity and the life-span is fixed. The provision which Allah gives a man is a trust for which he will be held to account. It makes a believer behave as Allah wills: he runs in the remembrance of Allah but walks in this world; he is moderate in the quest for wealth and its acquisition and takes it from what is lawful and does not commit acts of disobedience to obtain it. O Allah, provide us with contentment, certainty, and pleasure in what You have allotted for us so that we may be the wealthiest of people by Your bounty and mercy!

Exercising caution with respect to love of wealth and desire for it

This point is closely connected to the previous one. Indeed they are like Siamese twins which cannot be separated. Wealth has a stronger and more damaging effect than even that of wine. From the cradle to the grave the self is always hankering after more and more property and wealth. That is why the Messenger, may Allah bless him and grant him peace, explained to us that there is an

94

aspect of human nature which constantly incites us to love of wealth and eagerness for it. He has called on us to be very careful indeed about allowing this characteristic to master our feelings and behaviour, saying, "The hearts of old men are sullied by love of two things: love of life and love of wealth." Al-Bukhari and Muslim related this from Abu Hurayra.

This is why the Messenger, may Allah bless him and grant him peace, used to seek refuge with Allah from "a self which is not satisfied" because he saw that the avidity produced by a fierce desire for increase of wealth represents a terrible danger for the heart and *deen* of man to the extent that setting hungry wolves loose in a peaceful flock of sheep to rend their flesh and devour them is less harmful and will do less damage than man's burning greed to amass wealth will do to his *deen*. The Noble Qur'an makes this abundantly clear to us in various places where it talks of the destruction of individuals who loved wealth inordinately.

At the head of them was Qarun. Allah gave him treasures, the keys to which alone were too heavy for a group of strong men to carry, let alone the treasures themselves. In spite of that, he did not praise Allah nor thank him for His bounty and act righteously. Arrogance and love of wealth made him blind to his misguidance. So he was one of the people who were destroyed as an admonition and a lesson for everyone who loves wealth and is eager for it and does not oppose the avarice and greed of his lower self.

> "Qarun was one of the people of Musa and he was overweening towards them. We gave him treasures, the keys to which alone made up a heavy load for a group of strong men. When his people said to him, 'Do not exult. Allah does not love people who exult. Seek, with what Allah has given you, the Abode of the Next World, not forgetting your portion of this world. And do good as Allah has been good to you. And do not desire corruption in the earth. Allah does not love people who corrupt.' He said, 'I have only been given it on account of a knowledge I possess.' Did he not know that before him Allah destroyed other generations greater in strength than him and greater in gathered wealth? The evildoers will not be questioned*

here about their misdeeds. He went out among his people in his finery. Those who desired the life of this world said, 'Oh! If only we had the same as has been given to Qarun! What immense good fortune he possesses!' But those who had been given knowledge said, 'Woe to you! Allah's reward is better for him who believes and acts rightly. But none will receive it except for the steadfast.' We caused the earth to swallow up both him and his house. There was no group to come to his support besides Allah, and he was not one of those who receive support. Those who had longed to be in his place the day before woke up that morning saying, 'Allah expands His provision to any of His slaves He wills, or restricts it. Had Allah not been gracious to us, He would have caused us to be swallowed up as well. Ah! Truly the rejectors are not successful.' That Abode of the Next World We assign to those who do not seek exaltation in the earth or corruption. The end result is for the godfearing." (28:76-83)

The second example which Allah gives us as an admonition and lesson against love of wealth, a love which blinds people to the truth of Allah, His Way and the *Shari'a*, is the story of the owners of a garden which they inherited from their father. They were beguiled by its ripe fruits and their burning greed led them to want to monopolise their good fortune and prevent the poor and destitute from taking the share which Allah had allotted them, despite the fact that their believing father had always undertaken this duty. He used to give the extra fruit to them.

How very wrong they were! When divine justice is abandoned because greed is given free rein, the avaricious people concerned create havoc in the earth and encourage others to be avaricious as well, and then the poor become destitute because of the greed of the wealthy. The vengeance of Allah is near at hand and He makes an object lesson of those people who are diseased with love of wealth, so that they become an admonition and lesson for all people of intelligence. Allah's decision is final. *"When He desires a thing, He merely says to it, 'Be' and it is."* (36:82) So as soon as night came, a fierce wind arose and made the garden like burnt land, stripped bare. Morning found the garden's owners repentant and ruined, a suitable penalty for their plot to deprive the poor. Allah Almighty says in His Immense Qur'an:

"We have tried them as We tried the owners of the garden when they swore that they would harvest in the morning but did not say the redeeming words, 'If Allah wills'. So a visitation from your Lord came to it while they slept and in the morning it was like burnt land, stripped bare. In the morning they called out to one another, 'Leave early for your land if you are going to pick.' So they set off, quietly saying to one another, 'Do not let any poor man into it today while you are there.' They left early, intent on carrying out their scheme. But when they saw it, they said, 'We have missed our way. No, the truth is that we are destitute.' The best of them said, 'Did I not say to you, "Why do you not glorify Allah?"' They said, 'Glory be to our Lord! Truly we have been wrongdoers.' They turned to face each other in mutual blame. They said, 'Woe to us! We were indeed immoderate. Maybe our Lord will give us something better than it in exchange. We make entreaty to our Lord.' Such is the punishment. And the punishment of the Next World is much greater, if they did but know." (68:17-33)

The third example is that of a Muslim who was contemporary with the Messenger, may Allah bless him and grant him peace. His love of wealth was so intense that it moved him to ask the Messenger to make a supplication for him that Allah would enrich him from His bounty. The Messenger tried to treat this psychological illness by making it clear that a little for which there is thankfulness is better than a lot for which one cannot be thankful enough. However, the wily self which commands to evil drove this man to the path of destruction. He tried to justify his desire by clothing it in pious platitudes, saying that wealth in the hand of the believer is a great blessing which he can spend on the poor and destitute.

The Messenger, may Allah bless him and grant him peace, was finally forced to allow him to continue on his self-destructive way so that he would be a warning for other believers. After doing everything he could to warn the man, the Prophet eventually prayed to Allah to enrich him; and the ensuing wealth did indeed prove to be evil for its owner since it first distracted him from the group prayer and then from the *Jumu'a* until finally Allah sealed his heart and he became one of the hypocrites who say one thing but believe another. This is the worst kind of loss because the hypocrites are in the lowest level of the Fire. It is a frightening lesson and is an eloquent reminder for us of the terrible end of those who devote themselves tirelessly to the acquisition of wealth. What is the use of all the treasures of this world if a man loses his own self and squanders the teachings of his Lord?

> *"Some of them contracted with Allah: 'If He gives us some of His overflowing favour, we will then give* sadaqa *and be among the righteous.' But when He did give them some of His overflowing favour, they were mean with it and turned away, disclaiming. As a result He has punished them by putting hypocrisy in their hearts until the day they meet Him, because they failed Allah in what they had promised Him and because they lied. Do they not know that Allah knows their secrets and their private talk, and that Allah is the Knower of all unseen things?"* (9:75-77)

O Allah! Do not make this world our major concern and do not put love of wealth into our hearts so that it veils us from the Next World! Fill our hearts with true wealth. You have power over everything and are the Answerer of prayers.

The necessity of earning money from lawful sources

Lawfulness is the primary factor that makes wealth acceptable and worthy of respect. All wealth which does not come by lawful means is harmful for its owner. Some people think that if a person does good with his unlawful wealth and dubious earnings that will act as a reparation and remove the stigma of unlawfulness from it. That is very far indeed from the *Shari'a*. The Messenger, may Allah bless him and grant him peace, was very eager to open our eyes to the danger of all earnings from dubious sources and he was very concerned to encourage love of the lawful and respect for the legitimate in our hearts. So listen, my Muslim brother, and make your heart attend to the words of the Prophet which will illuminate our hearts and our path so that we can proceed on the path of life with steady steps, seeking the pleasure of Allah and His Messenger.

Abu Hurayra, may Allah be pleased with him, related that the Messenger of Allah, may Allah bless him and grant him peace, said, "Allah is good and only accepts the good. Allah commands the believers to do the same things as He commands the Messengers. He says, *'O Messengers! Eat of the good things and act rightly. I most certainly know everything you do'* (23:51) and He says, *'O you who believe! Eat of the good things We have provided for you'* (2:172)." Then the Prophet mentioned a man who is on a long journey and is dusty and dishevelled. He stretches his hands towards heaven, saying, "O Lord! O Lord!" while his food is unlawful, his drink is unlawful, his clothes are unlawful and he is nourished by the unlawful. How can such a person have his supplication answered?

Anas, may Allah be pleased with him, related that the Prophet, may Allah bless him and grant him peace, said, "Seeking the lawful is obligatory for every Muslim."

'Abdullah ibn Mas'ud, may Allah be pleased with him, related that the Prophet, may Allah bless him and grant him peace, said, "Seeking the lawful is an obligation in addition to the other obligations."

It is related that Ibn 'Abbas, may Allah be pleased with him, said, "This *ayat* was recited in the presence of the Messenger of Allah, may Allah bless him and grant him peace: *'O Mankind! Eat what is good and lawful on the earth'* (2:168). Sa'd ibn Abi Waqqas, may Allah be pleased with him, stood up and said, 'Messenger of Allah, ask Allah to make me someone whose supplication is answered.' The Prophet said to him, 'Sa'd, make your food good and you will have your supplication answered. By the

One who has the soul of Muhammad in His hand, if a slave puts a morsel of the unlawful into his stomach, no action is accepted from him for forty days. The Fire is more entitled to anyone whose flesh has been nurtured by ill-gotten wealth.'"

It is related that 'Ali, may Allah be pleased with him, said, "Once we were sitting with the Messenger of Allah, may Allah bless him and grant him peace, when a man from the people of al-'Aliyya came up to us and said, 'Messenger of Allah, tell me what is the hardest thing in this *deen* and the easiest thing.' He said, 'The easiest thing is the testimony that there is no god but Allah and Muhammad is His slave and Messenger. The hardest thing, my brother from al-'Aliyya, is trustworthiness. There is no *deen* for the one who has no trustworthiness, and no prayer and no *zakat*. My brother from al-'Aliyya, whoever gets some money from what is unlawful and then puts on a shirt bought with it, his prayer is not accepted from him until he removes that shirt. Allah Almighty is too noble and majestic, my brother of al-'Aliyya, to accept his action or prayer while he is wearing a shirt bought with what is unlawful.'"

Abu Hurayra, may Allah be pleased with him, related that the Prophet, may Allah bless him and grant him peace, said, "Anyone who buys something stolen knowing that it is stolen has shared in its dishonour and sin."

He also related that the Prophet, may Allah bless him and grant him peace, said, "When you pay the *zakat* on your property, you have discharged your duty. But anyone who amasses unlawful wealth and then gives it as *sadaqa* receives no reward and still bears the burden of the sin involved."

Abu Dawud related in *al-Marasil* that al-Qasim ibn Mukhaymira, may Allah be pleased with him, said that the Messenger of Allah, may Allah bless him and grant him peace, said: "If anyone earns wealth through something sinful and gives it to his relatives or gives it as *sadaqa* or spends it in the Way of Allah, all of that will be gathered together and thrown into Jahannam."

Abu Hurayra, may Allah be pleased with him, related that the Messenger of Allah, may Allah bless him and grant him peace, said, "A time will come when people are not concerned whether what they have is lawful or unlawful." (Al-Bukhari and Muslim transmitted it.) Razin added in it: "On account of that their supplication is not answered."

Ibn 'Abbas, may Allah be pleased with him, related that the Messenger of Allah, may Allah bless him and grant him peace, said, "Do not envy anyone who amasses wealth from what is not lawful (or from something he has no right to). If he gives it as *sadaqa*, it is not accepted from him, and what he does not give away is his provision in the Fire."

Mu'adh, may Allah be pleased with him, related that the Prophet, may Allah bless him and grant him peace, said, "People will remain standing on the Day of Rising until they have been questioned about four things: how they spent their life, how they were tested in their youth, from where they earned their money and how they spent it, and their actions and what they did."

It is related from Ibn 'Imran that the Messenger of Allah, may Allah bless him and grant him peace, said, "This world is verdant and sweet. Whoever earns wealth from the lawful in it and spends it correctly, Allah will reward him for it and admit him to His Garden. Whoever earns wealth from what is not lawful and spends it improperly, Allah will admit him to the Abode of Humiliation. Many a person who acquires the wealth of Allah and His Messenger without discretion will be in the Fire on the Day of Rising. Allah says, '*Whenever it dies down, We will stoke up for them the Searing Blaze.* (17:97)"

Ka'b ibn 'Ujra, may Allah be pleased with him, said, "The Messenger of Allah, may Allah bless him and grant him peace, said to me, 'O Ka'b ibn 'Ujra! No flesh or blood nourished by ill-gotten wealth will enter the Garden. The Fire is more entitled to it. O Ka'b ibn 'Ujra, people return home in the evening: one person returns having ransomed his own self and set it free, whereas another returns having destroyed his own self.'"

In this way the Prophet reminded us of our responsibility regarding our wealth and set up the balance in the heart and conscience of the Muslim. In the question of wealth particularly you cannot afford to rely on anything which is unclear. Lawful sources are as clear as day and there is no excuse for anyone to consume anything unlawful. The lawful is clear and the unlawful is clearer still and more evident. O Allah! make our food lawful, our drink lawful, and our clothes lawful. Provide us with such lawful provision as will please You and make You pleased with us!

The prohibition of usury

The true believer is good and strives for good things and avoids all corrupt things. His flesh is not nourished by ill-gotten gains nor is his wealth increased by the unlawful. In the *Shari'a* the first and foremost of the disasters of wealth and property is the catastrophe of usury (*riba*). It is a heinous crime against which Islam takes a firm stance because it is an appetite which is hidden in the depths of the human self nourished by love of wealth. Man is prone to want to earn easy money rather than take risks and expend effort to obtain honest profit or cultivate the earth and gain his living by hard work. There is no doubt that usury is economically, politically and socially the most important issue facing the Muslims at this time and has proved the means by which the enemies of Islam have gained power over the Muslims and indeed the whole world. The fact that the last *ayats* of the Qur'an to be revealed by Allah were on the subject of usury and that Messenger of Allah, may Allah bless him and grant him peace, singled it out for mention in his *khutba* on 'Arafa during the Farewell Hajj - his final comprehensive statement of guidance for us - show us just how important it is for us.

The effects of usury, particularly in its most prevalent form of lending money at interest, are both pervasive and extremely destructive. In Britain alone, for instance, the staggering sum of several hundred billion pounds is owed by private individuals to credit companies, banks, stores, building societies and money lenders for consumer goods bought on credit. The human cost of this is increasing distress and discord in a great number of families and for many absolute despair at not being able to make ends meet, leading to a growing number of suicides. On the international scene, the situation is the same or even worse. In many countries the gross national product is not sufficient to pay even the interest on the money that has been borrowed, let alone the capital, which means that everyone in those countries is working for foreign banks. The situation is appalling and this is just the tip of the iceberg. The underlying effects of usury have corrupted every aspect of human life in subtle ways that are not immediately obvious but which can be traced directly back to the introduction and practice of usury. Usury is a poison which pollutes all it touches. Its prohibition in the Qur'an leaves no room for doubt. The Almighty says:

> "O you who believe! Fear Allah and forgo any remaining usury if you are believers. If you do not, know that it means war from Allah and His Messenger. If you turn in repentance you may have your capital, not wronging and not being wronged. If someone is in difficulties, there should be a postponement until things are easier. But making it a free gift would be better for you if you did but know. Fear a Day on which you will be returned to Allah. Then every self will be paid in full for what it earned. They will not be wronged." (2:278-281)

> "O you who believe! Do not feed on usury, multiplied and then remultiplied. Fear Allah so that perhaps you will be successful. Fear the Fire which has been prepared for those who reject. Obey Allah and the Messenger so that perhaps you will gain mercy." (3:130-132)

My brother Muslim, take note also of this detailed reminder from the *hadiths* of the Prophet which expound, detail and clarify what is contained in the basic code of the Noble Qur'an. This compilation of *hadiths* of the Prophet dispenses with discussion and silences every tongue because they are conclusive judgements articulated not from personal opinion but by inspiration from Allah, the Almighty, the All-Powerful. Anyone who disobeys after hearing them has only himself to blame. The lawful is clear and the unlawful is clear, and between them are doubtful matters. Whoever avoids them has cleared himself in regard to his *deen* and his honour.

Abu Hurayra, may Allah be pleased with him, related that the Prophet, may Allah bless him and grant him peace, said, "Avoid the seven fatal sins." They said, "Messenger of Allah, what are they?" He said, "Making something else co-partner with Allah, sorcery, killing a soul which Allah has forbidden except by legal right, consuming usury, consuming the property of an orphan, fleeing on the day of battle, slandering careless chaste believing women."

Samura ibn Jundub, may Allah be pleased with him, related that the Prophet, may Allah bless him and grant him peace, said, "In the night I dreamt that two men came to me and took me to a holy land. We went on until we came to a river of blood in the middle of which there was a man standing and on the bank of the river there was another man with stones in front of him. The man in the river came forward; when he tried to get out, the other man threw a stone into his mouth and he went back to where he had been before. Whenever he tried to get out, the other man threw a stone into his mouth and he would go back to where he had been before. I asked, 'Who is this man I saw in the river?' He replied, 'Someone who consumed usury.'"

Jabir, may Allah be pleased with him, said, "The Messenger of Allah, may Allah bless him and grant him peace, cursed anyone who consumes usury, anyone who gives it, anyone who records it, and the witnesses to it."

Abu Hurayra, may Allah be pleased with him, related that the Messenger of Allah, may Allah bless him and grant him peace, said, "There are four to whom Allah has the right to refuse admittance to the Garden and forbid the taste of its bliss: someone who is addicted to wine, someone who consumes usury, someone who consumes the property of the orphan without any right, and someone who disobeys his parents."

It is related that Ibn 'Abbas said that the Messenger of Allah, may Allah bless him and grant him peace, said, "If anyone consumes a dirham of usury, it is like thirty-three acts of fornication for him. The Fire has the most right to anyone whose flesh is nourished from ill-gotten gains."

Al-Bara' ibn 'Azib, may Allah be pleased with him, said, "Usury has seventy-two doors, the least of which is equivalent to a man having intercourse with his mother. One of the worst forms of usury is for a man to detract from his brother's honour."

Ibn 'Abbas said: "The Messenger of Allah, may Allah bless him and grant him peace, forbade fruits to be sold until they were ripe, and he declared, 'When fornication and usury appear in a place, then its people have opened themselves up to the punishment of Allah."

Al-Isbahani related from Abu Sa'id al-Khudri, may Allah be pleased with him, that when the Messenger of Allah, may Allah bless him and grant him peace, ascended to Heaven, there were some men with bellies as huge as houses. Their bellies hung down... They stand at the Fire every morning and evening, saying, 'Our Lord, do not let the Hour ever come!' I said, 'Jibril, who are they?' He replied, 'They are the people of your community who consumed usury. They only rise as someone driven mad by the touch of Shaytan.'"

Ibn Mas'ud, may Allah be pleased with him, related that the Prophet, may Allah bless him and grant him peace, said, "Before the Hour, the practice of usury, fornication and wine-drinking will be open and public."

It is related that 'Awf ibn Malik, may Allah be pleased with him, said that the Messenger of Allah, may Allah bless him and grant him peace, said "Beware of the sins which are not forgiven. One of them is misappropriation. Whoever misappropriates anything will bring it on the Day of Rising. There is also consuming usury. Anyone who consumes usury will rise on the Day of Rising like a madman touched by insanity. Then He recited, *'Those who practise usury will not rise except as someone struck mad by the touch of Shaytan'* (2:275)."

'Abdullah ibn Mas'ud, may Allah be pleased with him, related that the Prophet, may Allah bless him and grant him peace, said, "Even though the profit of usury be much, it will lead in the end to penury."

Abu Hurayra, may Allah be pleased with him, said that the Messenger of Allah, may Allah bless him and grant him peace, said. "A time will come when there will be no one who does not consume usury. Even if he does not consume it, its dust will alight on him.'"

It is related from Abu Umama, may Allah be pleased with him, that the Prophet, may Allah bless him and grant him peace, said, "There will be a people of this community who will spend the night eating and drinking, diverting themselves and playing, and by the morning they will have been turned into apes and pigs. The earth will swallow them up and spit them out so that people will say in the morning, 'The tribe of so-and-so were swallowed by the earth in the night. The house of so-and-so was swallowed up by the earth in the night.' Stones will be sent down on them from heaven as they were sent down on the people of Lut, on their people and houses. The barren wind which destroyed 'Ad will be sent against them, against their people and houses, because of their drinking wine, wearing silk, engaging women singers, consuming usury and disassociating themselves from their kin."

You spoke the truth, Messenger of Allah. You conveyed the message and carried out the trust and counselled the community and removed all sorrow. Whoever is guided has been guided to his own good and will obtain the good of this world and the Next. Whoever is misguided has clearly wronged his own self and enveloped it in evil and directed it to the deepest depths of the fires of this world and the Next. This is not a fitting end for someone with intelligence who knows his Lord and listens to the guidance of His Messenger and is illuminated by the light of Islam.

Usury is easy money followed by clear loss which is not deferred to what happens after death. Its consequences are felt in this life since it destroys the foundations of society with an effectiveness unmatched by any other cause. Therefore Islam has forbidden it because of the intensity of its destructive effects and set out other rules for the circulation of wealth in Muslim society, which spread progress and affluence in it and achieve for its individuals the comfort and security they seek and present a solution to the difficulties now facing all the people of the earth.

The prohibition of hoarding

A hoarder is someone who hoards away in his warehouses things like food and clothing which people need in order to sell them on the black market for exorbitant prices. He is cursed and the curse will continue to afflict his wealth until it turns to dust, even if that takes a long time. The Messenger, may Allah bless him and grant him peace, said, "An importer may prosper but a hoarder is cursed." Ibn Maja transmitted this from 'Umar, may Allah be pleased with him. An importer is the opposite of a hoarder because he imports what people need from distant or neighbouring lands and then makes them available to people at reasonable prices which do not burden them and do not make them gasp at the rise in price. Reasonable prices are desired by the hearts of most consumers because they enable them to get what they need within the means at their disposal. Islam desires to make life easy for people and to make sure they are able to get what they need for their subsistence. That is why the Messenger, may Allah bless him and grant him peace, censured those who hoard, saying, "Evil is he who hoards. If Allah lowers prices, he grieves. If He raises them, he exults." At-Tabarani related this from Mu'adh.

The mere fact of being sad at a decrease in prices and happy when they rise indicates a base covetous soul which exults in the sorrow of others and is unhappy when they are happy. This is contrary to the basic principles of belief which makes the Muslims like a single body in their mutual love and mercy. When one limb complains, the rest of the body prays for it with sleeplessness and fever. It also makes the Muslims like a single building whose parts reinforce one another. But the soul of the hoarder desires wealth with a passion which makes him take it as a god. It dominates his dealings and defines his behaviour

A man who is pleased with Allah as his Lord, Islam as his *deen*, and Muhammad, may Allah bless him and grant him peace, as his Prophet and Messenger will humble his heart to the *Shari'a* of Allah. His own desires will be made subservient to what the Beloved Prophet brought. The Messenger gave people the strongest possible encouragement to keep the sources of provision as far as possible from any chicanery or conspiracy. Any merchant involved in hoarding and withholding these provisions or with increasing prices will not find any part in the abundance of Allah or that of His Messenger, for he has washed his hands of Allah and Allah has consequently washed His hands of him. We seek refuge with Allah!

Food is not the only commodity whose hoarder was promised punishment by the Messenger and hoarding is not the only practice which brings ruin and the curse on the one who does it. Simple haggling and bidding against one another which leads to inflated prices in something staple, something which people need in their daily life, puts the perpetrator into a deep pit of Allah's anger and punishment.

Look at these noble *hadiths* of the Prophet which overflow with wisdom but also overflow with fury and vengefulness towards on those who make doing injury to others a means to obtaining wealth and property. You should beware and be warned by those before you who were ruled by the appetite for wealth and so withheld the means of provision and the keys of life for the Muslim community.

Ibn 'Umar, may Allah be pleased with both of them, said that the Messenger of Allah, may Allah bless him and grant him peace, said, "If anyone hoards grain for forty days, he has washed his hands of Allah and Allah has washed His hands of him. If someone goes hungry among the people of any place, they have washed their hands of the protection of Allah Almighty."

Abu Umama, may Allah be pleased with him, related that the Messenger of Allah, may Allah bless him and grant him peace, said, "The people of the cities are confined in the way of Allah. Foodstuffs should not be hoarded and withheld from them and prices should not be raised for them. If anyone were to withhold from them for forty days and then to give it all away as *sadaqa*, that would not act as expiation for him."

Abu Hurayra and Ma'qil ibn Yasar said that the Messenger of Allah, may Allah bless him and grant him peace, said, "Hoarders and murderers will be gathered on the same level. If anyone interferes with any of the prices of the Muslims with the aim of inflating them, it is a duty for Allah to punish him in the Fire on the

Day of Rising."

Ibn 'Umar, may Allah be pleased with him and his father, said that the Messenger of Allah, may Allah bless him and grant him peace, said, "Hoarding food in Makka is heresy!"

Abu Hurayra, may Allah be pleased with him, related that the Messenger of Allah, may Allah bless him and grant him peace, said, "Anyone who hoards something intending to make its price rise for the Muslims commits an offence and has washed his hands of the protection of Allah."

Al-Haytham ibn Rafi' related from Abu Yahya al-Makki from Farrukh, the client of 'Uthman ibn 'Affan, that some food was left at the door of the mosque. 'Umar ibn al-Khattab, may Allah be pleased with him, who was the Amir al-Mu'minin at that time, went out and said, "What is this food?" They said, "Some food which was brought to us." He said, "May Allah bless it and the one who brought it to us." One of those who were with him said, "Amir al-Mu'minin, it was hoarded." He said, "Who hoarded it?" They said, "It was hoarded by Farrukh and a client of 'Umar ibn al-Khattab." He sent for them and when they were brought, he said, "What led you to hoard the food of the Muslims?" They said, "Amir al-Mu'minin, we buy and sell with our money." 'Umar said, "I heard the Messenger of Allah, may Allah bless him and grant him peace, say, 'If anyone keeps food from the Muslims, Allah will afflict him with leprosy and bankruptcy.'" At that, Farrukh said, "Amir al-Mu'minin, I make a pledge with Allah and I make a pledge with you that I will never hoard food again." He moved to Egypt. As for 'Umar's client, he said, "We buy and sell with our money." Abu Yahya states that he saw 'Umar's client with leprosy.

The reasons for the Islamic prohibition of hoarding

Hoarding consists in buying up and storing large quantities of a particular merchandise from its producers and inevitably leads to a decrease of that merchandise in the market and sometimes even to its disappearance, which forces consumers to pay high prices to obtain their needs. This leads to a chain reaction of increase in prices which is known as inflation. The disadvantages of inflation are not hidden from anyone. They can be very briefly summed up under these principal points:

- The weakening of people's trust in the national currency which can lead to a flight from money because of the loss in its real value due to the rise in prices.

- Poor allocation of economic resources owing to the channelling of capital into areas of economic activity which achieve the greatest possible profit without any consideration of their role in satisfying people's basic needs.

- The weakening of the ability to export because the rise in prices leads to a rise in the cost of production which leads to goods not being able to compete with the prices of other goods in the world market.

- The creation of a suitable climate and fertile ground for speculation which exacerbates the problem of misallocation of economic resources, these being directed to areas where they will achieve a quick profit without any attention being paid to the needs of the people.

- The deepening of social imbalances as a result of the decrease in real income for people with fixed wages, and an increase in the profitability of other kinds of business which leads to a marked increase in the disparity of the distribution of wealth and national income. This has a negative effect on the level of political and social stability in a country.

- The spread of a love for quick wealth which is prompted by price increases. This is inevitably accompanied by lack of mutual solidarity and concern between different classes of society and the consequent destruction of social solidarity because of the anxiety and bitterness which people feel.

Islam has forbidden hoarding because of all of these evil effects. It is an illness which afflicts societies in their livelihood, character, and balance. It is not likely that the divine Message containing the final guidance for all human beings would neglect to provide a remedy for this illness which has such an effect on human life; and indeed Islam treats it in all its aspects, inwardly and outwardly, in counsel and guidance, with supervision and prosecution. The authority of the ruler and the force of the law are invoked to deter and punish hoarding. Islam makes the adequate supply of goods in the markets equal to *jihad* in the Way of Allah. *Jihad* is nothing but preservation of the land and its goods and helping people to follow the Straight Path. That is why the Noble Messenger, may Allah bless him and grant him peace, said, "Give the good news that someone who imports to our market is the same as someone who does *jihad* in the Way of Allah. Someone who hoards in our market is like someone who is a renegade in the Way of Allah."

The punishment of hoarders in Islam

In view of the danger that hoarding, which is the exploitation of people's needs to achieve higher profits, will lead to price rises, Islam has not left the regulation of this matter in human hands. That is because it goes beyond individual harm and causes harm to society as a whole and the corruption of its practices. Corruption of society, generally speaking, is caused by wilful deviation from the *Shari'a* of Allah and His Messenger, and the punishment for this is severe. That is why the *fuqaha'* of the Muslims have agreed to fight and oppose hoarding, especially during times when people need the goods that are being hoarded. The war against hoarding is carried out by implementing the following positive measures:

- The hoarder must sell his goods at a fair price. If he refuses, the Qadi will sell them for him.

- The hoarder is awarded a discretionary punishment which is a punishment imposed by the *muhtasib*. Ibn al-Qayyim said about this, "A discretionary punishment varies according to the exigencies of the time, place or situation. The severity of the punishment varies according to the seriousness of the crime and the inveterateness of the criminal." The punishment might be imprisonment, beating or a fine which are the penalties usually imposed for the crimes of hoarding or pricing violations.

That is how Islam deals with hoarding, which is one of the calamities resulting from an excessive desire for wealth. It is a remedy which encompasses spirit and body, admonition and punishment. Truly Islam takes everything into consideration and governs every aspect of life.

The prohibition of cheating

Cheating is a way of obtaining money and property by unlawful means. Sometimes the desire for wealth outweighs all other principles and values and people resort to cheating in order to sell their goods. Cheating is one of the crimes most liable to be explained away, excused and justified. It is very easy for a man to delude himself that what he has done is not unlawful when he has not actually stolen and not forced his victim to do what he wants. This is why the Prophet, may Allah bless him and grant him peace, is concerned to stir the dormant conscience. He, may the blessings and peace of my Lord be upon him, said, "An evil person is one who makes unlawful things lawful by sophisms."

Cheating is in fact the same as simple theft. In the same way that people dislike to be cheated in any transaction they undertake or goods they buy, and they make sure of the soundness of what they receive, it is obligatory for them to be equally particular in their own case and make certain that they are not cheating or deceiving others. The Prophet, peace and blessings be upon him, said, "Anyone who cheats us is not one of us. The crafty man and the swindler are in the Fire." At-Tabarani related this from Ibn Mas'ud.

The connection made here between cheating, swindling and craftiness cuts the ground from under the feet of those who use their malicious cleverness first to cheat people and then to persuade themselves that they have not done anything wrong or committed any sin. Those who amass or increase their wealth by cheating in whatever form or way have no place in the rightly-guided ranks of the community. The first thing that rightly-guided believers adorn themselves with is trustworthiness and faithfulness to each other's interests. The Prophet, may Allah bless him and grant him peace, said, "The believers are true to one another in friendship even if their houses and bodies are far apart. The dissolute are true to one another in treachery even if their houses and bodies are close together." The father of Ibn Hibban related this from Anas ibn Malik.

Indeed, faithfulness is one of the clearest signs of belief. In places where temptation is great it has even more worth and the necessity for it is even more felt. Investigating the validity of things and specifying their faults and shortcomings is not an duty to be entrusted to one particular public servant but is rather a social and communal duty addressed to all those who believe in their Lord and listen to the Words of their Lord and answer the call of the Truth.

This assortment of noble *hadiths* of the Prophet will diffuse their sweet scent on the Path of Light and serve to guide the misguided and take the hand of all those who are confused and lost.

Abu Hurayra, may Allah be pleased with him, said that the Messenger of Allah, may Allah bless him and grant him peace, passed by a heap of grain and put his hand in it, and his fingers felt moistness. He said, "You with the grain, what is this?" He said, "The rain caught it, Messenger of Allah." He said, "So why didn't you put it on top of the rest so that people could see it? Anyone who cheats us is not one of us."

Anas ibn Malik, may Allah be pleased with him, said: "The Messenger of Allah, may Allah bless him and grant him peace, came out to us in the market and saw some grain in a heap. He put his hand in it and brought out moist grain which had been caught by the rain. He said to the owner, 'What made you do this?' The man said, 'By the One who sent you with the truth, it is the same grain.' He asked, 'Why didn't you put the wet to one side and the dry to one side and sell what you know is sound? Anyone who cheats us is not one of us.'"

Qays ibn Abi Gharaza said, "The Prophet, may Allah bless him and grant him peace, passed by a man selling grain and said, "You with the grain, is the bottom of this the same as the top?' He said, 'Yes, Messenger of Allah.' The Messenger of Allah said, 'Anyone who cheats the Muslims is not one of them.'"

'Uqba ibn 'Amir, may Allah be pleased with him, related that the Prophet, may Allah bless him and grant him peace, said, "A Muslim is the brother of a Muslim. When a Muslim sells something containing a fault to his brother, it is not lawful for him to fail to point it out."

Tamim ad-Dari, may Allah be pleased with him, related that the Messenger of Allah, may Allah bless him and grant him peace, said, "The *deen* is faithfulness." We said, "To whom, Messenger of Allah?" He said, "To Allah, His Messenger, the leaders of the believers and their common people."

Hudhayfa ibn al-Yaman, may Allah be pleased with him, related that the Messenger of Allah, may Allah bless him and grant him peace, said, "Anyone who is not concerned with the affairs of the Muslims is not one of them. Anyone who does not pass the night and day in faithfulness to Allah, His Messenger, His Book, his leader, and the common Muslims is not one of them."

Anas, may Allah be pleased with him, related that the Prophet, may Allah bless him and grant him peace, said, "None of you is a real believer until he loves for his brother what he loves for himself."

Thus the merciful Messenger encouraged us always to be on our guard against the pitfalls of cheating. He wants to free us from the temptation experienced by the desires of the lower self in the matter of buying and selling. He puts us on guard against anything dubious which might tempt us to unlawful profit. Earning money by means of cheating is a quick way to ruin and perdition, even if it appears to be a way of getting more. O Allah, safeguard us in the same way that You safeguarded Your righteous friends and god-fearing slaves! You are the best Master and the best Helper.

The prohibition against tampering with weights and measures

Just as Islam forbids falsifying any type of goods by cheating, it also firmly forbids giving short weight and measure. The sin of stinting has been latent in the depths of the human soul through the ages because it is a short cut to quick and easy money by means of theft through giving short measure and weight. This is what the Messengers fought against in their summons to liberate human souls from their enslavement to matter and open them to the worship of Allah. The Almighty says in His Generous Book:

"And to Madyan their brother Shu'ayb. He said, 'O my people! Worship Allah. You have no god other than Him. Do not give short measure and weight. I see you doing well and I fear for you the punishment of an encircling day. O my people! Give full measure and weight with justice, do not deprive people of what belongs to them, and do not go about the earth, corrupting it. What remains with Allah is better for you if you are believers. I am not set over you as a keeper.'" (11:84-85)

"Give full measure when you measure and weigh with a level balance. That is better and gives the best result." (17:35)

"He erected heaven and established the balance, so that you would not overstep in the balance. Give just weight; do not skimp in the balance." (55:7-9)

"Woe to the stinters: those who, when they measure against people, take full measure, but when they measure or weigh for them, give less than is due! Do those people not realise that they are going to be raised up on a Mighty Day, the Day all people stand before the Lord of all the worlds?" (83:1-6)

"We sent Our Messengers with the clear Signs and sent down with them the Book and the Balance so that people might establish justice." (57:25)

115

Islam encourages the establishment of balance in life in the strongest possible terms. Imbalance in business dealings causes an imbalance in society as a whole because it entails injustice and encroaching on people's rights. Injustice will be darkness on the Day of Rising because it is one of the most heinous of sins. Allah has accorded various rights to any person who is wronged, the greatest of which is that there is no veil between his supplication and Allah.

We cannot find anything more terrifying than those statements of the Prophet which depict the terrors that await those who give short measure and weight and describe the abyss which awaits nations and peoples when that foul disease is prevalent among them.

Ibn 'Abbas, may Allah be pleased with him, related that the Messenger of Allah, may Allah bless him and grant him peace, said to people using weights and measures, "You are dealing with a matter for which nations before you were destroyed."

Ibn 'Umar, may Allah be pleased with him and his father, said, "The Messenger of Allah, may Allah bless him and grant him peace, came to us and said, 'O company of Emigrants! There are five evils by which you may be tested - and I seek refuge with Allah from them ever reaching you: promiscuity does not appear in a people to the extent that they are open about it without the plague spreading among them as well as other diseases which did not occur among their forebears who have passed away. People do not give short measure and weight without being afflicted by droughts, great trouble and governmental tyranny. People do not refuse to pay the *zakat* of their property without being denied rain from heaven. Were it not for the beasts, they would not have any water at all. People do not break the contract of Allah and His Messenger without Allah giving an enemy power over them who takes some of what they possess. The leaders of the Muslims do not cease to judge by the Book of Allah and rule by what Allah has revealed without Allah making trouble between them.'"

Ibn Mas'ud, may Allah be pleased with him said, "Fighting in the Way of Allah expiates all sins except for breach of trust." Then he said, "A slave will be brought on the Day of Rising. Even if he fought in the way of Allah, he will be asked, 'What about your trust?' He will say, 'O Lord, how is that possible when the world has departed?' It will be said, 'Take him to the Pit.' He will be taken to the Pit and then his trust will appear before him in the form it had on the day he was given it. He will see it and recognise it and he will rush after it until he catches it. He will carry it on his shoulders. When he looks and supposes that he has got out, it will slip from his shoulders and he will chase after it until he catches it. This will go on forever." Then he said, "The prayer is a trust. *Wudu'* is a trust. The weight is a trust. The measure is a trust." He listed several things and the most important of them was deposits. I went to al-Bara' ibn 'Azib and said, "Do you hear what Ibn Mas'ud has been saying?' He said, "It is as he stated. He spoke the truth. Haven't you heard Allah say, *'Allah commands you to return to their owners the things you hold on trust*" (4:58). (Al-Bayhaqi)

Islam demands of all earning that it be lawful without any fraudulence or any shortening of weight or measure, because deviation from the path of truth will cause a person to slip into the lower levels of sin until his sin encompasses him and drowns him in the seas of the great abyss from which there is no rescue.

The prohibition against making false oaths

One of the greatest sins resulting from the love of amassing money is the sin of making false oaths in order to obtain something to which you have no right.

Ibn Mas'ud, may Allah be pleased with him, said, "Anyone who swears an oath to get hold of some property belonging to a Muslim to which he has no right will meet Allah and find Him angry with him. The Messenger of Allah, may Allah bless him and grant him peace, recited to us confirmation of this from the Book of Allah, the Mighty and Majestic: *'Those who sell Allah's contract and their own oaths for a paltry price...'* (3:77)."

'Abdullah ibn 'Amr ibn al-'As related that the Prophet, may Allah bless him and grant him peace, said, "The major sins are: making something else co-partner with Allah, disobeying parents, and making false oaths."

'Abdu'r-Rahman ibn 'Awf, may Allah be pleased with him, related that the Prophet, may Allah bless him and grant him peace, said, "False oaths diminish wealth."

The Prophet also said, "The best form of earning is that of merchants who do not lie when they speak, do not betray when they are trusted, do not break their promises when they make them, are not censured when they buy or praised when they sell, and are not oppressive in claiming what they are due." Al-Bayhaqi transmitted it from Mu'adh ibn Jabal.

Making sure your wealth is wholesome and withholding your evil from other people is not just a matter of avoiding cheating, hoarding, giving short measure and weight and not making false oaths. It also entails avoiding trade involving anything which Allah has made unlawful - unlawful food, unlawful drink and unlawful goods. Trading in anything that is forbidden and unlawful gives rise to improper earnings and impure wealth. That is why Islam has absolutely forbidden it and cautioned against it. A true believer is good and strives for good and avoids the bad. His flesh is not nourished by ill-gotten gains nor is his wealth increased by anything unlawful, for he believes in Allah and His Messenger. Islam prohibits people from indulging the base desires and appetites to which they are naturally inclined and so saves them from the fires of this world and the Next and impels them towards all that is pleasing to Allah and His Messenger.

The prohibition of theft and misappropriation

Allah Almighty says in His Noble Book:

"O you who believe! Do not consume one another's property by false means, but only by means of mutually agreed trade." (4:29)

In this context "false means" include all the kinds of unlawful earning forbidden in Islam which we have been discussing above and also includes misappropriation (*ghulul*) which comprises pilfering and stealing public property. Misappropriation is not only theft and unlawful earning but also pernicious sabotage and flagrant treachery because it is violating public property which is not owned by any individual but by the whole community. It belongs to all the people and the majority of them work for it. Lack of control tempts the eyes and stimulates the appetite of love of wealth. When temptation is transformed into action then the breach swiftly widens and thieving and embezzling hands proliferate. Then public property - which is the right of widows, the weak, workers, orphans, invalids and the destitute - disappears. That which supports the best interests of the community and supplies the necessities of their lives simply disappears. This public wealth becomes the object of embezzlement, misappropriation and dissipation. If people only knew the right of inviolability which public property has, no one would dare to misappropriate it. This does not only apply to money but to everything that is considered communal property.

Abu Hurayra, may Allah be pleased with him, said, "One day the Messenger of Allah, may Allah bless him and grant him peace, stood up among us and mentioned misappropriation: he declared it was a horrendous thing and that its punishment was terrible. He said, 'I would not like to find any of you coming on the Day of Rising with a complaining camel round his neck, saying, "O Messenger of Allah! Help me!" I will say, "I can do nothing for you now. I conveyed the message to you." I would not like to find any of you coming on the Day of Rising with a neighing horse around his neck, saying, "O Messenger of Allah! Help me!" I will say, "I can do nothing for you now. I conveyed the message to you." I would not like to find any of you coming on the Day of Rising with a bleating sheep round his neck, saying, "O Messenger of Allah! Help me!" I will say, "I can do nothing for you now. I conveyed the message to you." I would not like to find any of you coming on the Day of Rising with another soul crying out on his neck, saying, "O Messenger of Allah! Help me!" I will say, "I can do nothing for you now. I conveyed the message to you." I would not like to find any of you coming on the Day of Rising with rags fluttering on his neck, saying, "O Messenger of Allah! Help me!" I will say, "I can do nothing for you now. I conveyed the message to you." I would not like to find any of you coming on the Day of

Rising with gold and silver hanging on his neck, saying, "O Messenger of Allah! Help me!" I will say, "I can do nothing for you now. I conveyed the message to you." ' "

This noble *hadith* lists some of the things which constitute wealth. Any pilfering or embezzlement of things to which a man has no right will be a heavy burden which he will bear in this world and the Next; no one will be of any help to him against Allah because the Beloved Messenger advised the community and removed all our causes of grief. He fulfilled his task completely. No one can blame anyone after that except his own self which commands him to evil and to which he handed over the rein of appetites so that it guided him to the Fire.

The *hadiths* of the Messenger, may Allah bless him and grant him peace, which warn against theft and misappropriation are summed up in the incident involving the slave of Rifaʿa ibn Zayd who used to serve the Messenger of Allah after he became Muslim. In one of the expeditions he misappropriated a cloak for himself from the booty. Booty is public property. It is not correct for anyone to take anything from it until after it has been collected and divided according to the prescribed rules. That day Rifaʿa's slave was hit by a stray arrow from the enemy who ambushed the Muslims. The Messenger, may Allah bless him and grant him peace, heard his Companions praising him for achieving martyr-dom. He said, with sorrow showing in his face, "The cloak which he took from the booty has been set alight on his back."

How often the Prophet used to caution those of his Companions who acted as governors or were supervisors of public property! He made an example for them of a man he sent as a messenger to some people who misappropriated a woollen cloak. The Prophet said, "A like shirt of fire," meaning that he would be punished for what he did after his death by wearing a shirt of fire which would burn his spirit. It is related that ʿAwf ibn Malik said that the Messenger of Allah, may Allah bless him and grant him peace, said, "Beware of the sins which are not forgiven: misappropria-tion. Anyone who misappropriates something will carry it on the Day of Rising."

After reading these *hadiths* how can we still persist in error and indulging our appetites? If we do, we are in danger of being among those whose souls shout as loud as they can after they are dead, "Lord, send me back again so that I may act rightly!" The voices of the angels will respond: "Did not a clear warner from Allah come to you?"

Yes, O Lord, indeed Light and a Clear Book guiding to the Straight Path has come to us. Help us by Your bounty and generosity and magnanimity to remember You, thank You and worship You well.

Debts and debtors

Excess love of wealth leads to manifest problems where debt is concerned. The wealthy are often too mean to lend money to anyone in case they lose it or lose the opportunity to exploit it during the time it is in the possession of the debtor. A debtor, on the other hand, is eager for wealth at the time of his need but then lazy when it comes to repaying it, imagining this to be too much of a strain on him and fearing the poverty and need he was in which made him resort to borrowing in the first place. This is why Islam takes a middle position with regard to debt.

The rich are encouraged to satisfy the need of those in need and are given a great reward which is not obtained by their Muslim brothers. Thus Islam can be seen to be a *deen* of gallantry, manliness and social cohesion which fuses together society in the crucible of the belief with which Allah blessed us. But at the same time, it takes a firm stance towards anyone who is slow to repay his debts or who asks for a loan which he does not intend to repay. Wealth is the support of life. If it is left to the winds of idleness and wasteful consumption, the guideposts of life are lost. Lost along with them are those principles and values which are the basic building blocks on which the structure of societies is based. Islam is the *deen* of fulfilment of trusts and the *deen* of justice, equality, purity and giving people their rights. Allah Almighty says in His Noble Book:

"O you who believe! When you take on a debt for a specified period, write it down. A writer should write it down between you justly. No writer should refuse to write; seeing that Allah has taught him, he should write. The one incurring the debt should dictate and should fear Allah his Lord and not reduce it in any way. If the person incurring the debt is incompetent or weak or unable to dictate, then his guardian should dictate for him justly. Two men among you should act as witnesses. But if there are not two men, then a man and two women with whom you are satisfied as witnesses. Then if one of them forgets, the other can remind her. Witnesses should not refuse when they are called upon. Do not think it too trivial to write down, whether small or large, with the date that it falls due. Doing that is juster in Allah's sight and more helpful when bearing witness and more likely to eliminate any doubt. Unless it is an immediate transaction hand to hand, taken and given without delay: there is nothing blameworthy for you in not writing that down. Call witnesses when you trade. Neither writer nor witness should be put under pressure. If you do that, it is wanton deviation on your part. Fear Allah and Allah will teach you. Allah has knowledge of everything.

"If you are on a journey and cannot find a writer, something can be left as a security. If you leave things with one another on trust the one who is trusted must deliver up his trust and should fear Allah his Lord. Do not conceal testimony. If someone does conceal it, his heart has committed a crime. Allah knows everything you do." (2:282-283)

This is a precise arrangement for dealing with debt, containing a guarantee of rights and encouraging the spread of trust in communal financial relations. The "*ayat* of the debt" is the longest *ayat* in the Qur'an and a miracle for all times. Allah Almighty gives us instructions about recording debts, even if they are small, the necessity of integrity in respect of the obligation once it is recorded, and the rules of repayment and testimony. Integrity is a divine command which accompanies the Islamic creed. The Almighty says in His Noble Book:

> *"Be true to Allah's contract once you have made it, and do not break oaths once they are binding and you have made Allah your guarantee. Allah knows what you do."*
>
> (16:91)
>
> *"Fulfil your contracts. Contracts will be asked about."*
>
> (17:34)
>
> *"Allah will defend those who believe. Allah does not love any thankless traitor."* (22:39)

The importance of debts in Islam is such that Allah stipulates that the inheritance may only be distributed after all the debts of the deceased have first been settled:

> *"If you have brothers or sisters, your mother receives a sixth, after any bequest you make or any debts."* (4:11)
>
> *"If they have children, you receive a quarter of what they leave after any bequest they make or any debts. They receive a quarter of what you leave if you are childless. If you have children, they receive an eighth of what you leave after any bequest you make or any debts. If a man or woman has no direct heirs but has a brother or sister, each of them receives a sixth. If there are more than that, they share in a third after any non-prejudicial bequest you make or any debts. This is an instruction from Allah. Allah is All-Knowing, All-Forbearing."* (4:12)

After these details from the Noble Qur'an, we will now move on to the guidance of the noble Prophet on this matter. We will select some of the things he said about the relationship between creditors and debtors.

Abu Sa'id al-Khudri, may Allah be pleased with him, said, "I heard the Messenger of Allah, may Allah bless him and grant him peace, say, 'O Allah, I seek refuge with You from disbelief and debt.' A man asked, 'Messenger of Allah, do you equate disbelief with debt?' The Messenger said, 'Yes.'"

123

Here the Messenger, may Allah bless him and grant him peace, warns against debt in the strongest possible fashion so that those who prefer easy takings do not become dependent on borrowing and shun the path of effort, steadfastness, and perseverance. When borrowing becomes prevalent in any society, the spirit of communal trust is undermined and this results in a perversion in people's connection with money, diverting people from the path of good and mutual help in piety and fear of Allah to the path of avarice, meanness, and introversion. Islam strongly rejects long-term debt, especially when there is a conscious resolve to procrastinate or no intention to repay, indicating a desire to consume other peoples' property under false pretences. Allah cautions us against this in His Noble Qur'an as does His generous Messenger in his sublime guidance.

When the Messenger cautioned us against debt, he wanted people to be free of an oppressive worry which robs them of sleep, furrows their brows, and breaks their hearts. So he said, "Do not make your souls afraid after they have become secure." They said, "How is that, Messenger of Allah?" He replied, "By debt."

Imam Muslim related to us in his *Sahih* from Abu Hurayra, may Allah be pleased with him: "When a dead man was brought who had debts, the Messenger would ask, 'Has he left any surplus to settle his debts?' If he was told that he had left enough to cover his debts, he would pray over him. If he had not, he would say, 'Pray over your companion.' When Allah granted him victories, he said, 'I have more right to be the protector of the believers than themselves. If anyone dies leaving a debt, I will pay it. If anyone leaves property, it goes to his heirs.'"

The evident and grave responsibility of debt is clearly far-reaching. The Messenger, who is "merciful and compassionate to the believers," and has even more solicitude and sympathy and mercy and compassion for their dead, refrained from praying over a dead person with debts who had not left enough to cover his debts until Allah gave him a share from the booty of the victories. The first thing that he set out to do was to settle the debts of every Muslim who died owing a debt. This does not mean that debt is forbidden or unlawful. It is permitted under the condition of pressing need and a true resolve to repay it.

He, may Allah bless him and grant him peace, said, "If someone takes people's property intending to repay it, Allah will repay it for him. If someone takes people's property intending to ruin it, Allah will ruin him."

The Prophet said, "Anyone who has the intention to repay his debt will be helped by Allah."

The Messenger condemned any debt which puts people in situations of oppression, ruin and procrastination, and by which the Muslim disgraces his reputation, whereas Islam desires for him dignity and distinction and being connected to Allah and following His *Shari'a* and Way.

The Beloved Messenger did not want anyone to take on debt as a way of life or to make it one of the sources of his livelihood and provision, nor did he want debts to corrupt human relations whose aim is the highest degree of concord, love and trust. That is why procrastination in paying debts is hated. The Prophet, may Allah bless him and grant him peace, said, "The procrastination of the wealthy is injustice," meaning that for someone able to repay his debts to refuse to do so is iniquitous and sinful. A person has every right to pursue what he is owed. Allah does not desire injustice for people. *"Will the recompense for doing good be anything but goodness?"* If someone responds to a call for help and extends a helping hand to his brother by lending money to him, the debtor must return it once he is able to and fulfil the rights of his brother Muslim.

However, on the other hand we cannot help but see the gentleness of the Messenger, may Allah bless him and grant him peace, towards those debtors whose overwhelming circumstances forced them to incur debts and then made them unable to repay them. In this instance the Prophet of Mercy counselled compassion and advised granting a deferment to the one in difficulties - in other words, granting him a further delay and another opportunity to settle his debt without difficulty or hardship.

The Prophet said, "Among those before you there was a merchant who used give people credit. He used to say to his slaves,

'When you come to someone in difficulties, give him more time, perhaps Allah will pardon us.' Then Allah did pardon him."

The Prophet whom Allah sent as mercy to all the worlds said, "Whoever wishes Allah to save him from grief of the Day of Rising should relieve someone in difficulty or remit it from him."

Deferring the due date of repayment of a debt and extending it when someone is destitute and in difficulties is a magnanimous action for which Allah will give a great reward. Even more admirable is when the creditor absolves part or all of the debt of an insolvent debtor. This is how the Messenger upheld the balance with dazzling wisdom. He forbade people to become embroiled in debt and to consider that to be a wholesome state of affairs. But when circumstances forced people to resort to it, he made help easy for them. He enjoined on their creditors to go easy with them and promised them, in return for their mercy to the weak, the mercy of Allah, the Mighty and Powerful: the best reward and easement of grief on a Day which will be difficult for all mankind.

His kindness to debtors extended to teaching them how, in their powerlessness, they should knock at Allah's door and stand on the threshold of Divine Bounty asking for it to relieve them of the burdens and weights of debt.

One day the Prophet, may Allah bless him and grant him peace, entered the mosque outside the time of the prayer and found there a Companion who was one of the Ansar called Abu Umama. The Messenger asked, "Abu Umama, why do I see you sitting in the mosque outside the time of prayer?" Abu Umama said, "Worries and debts have bound me, Messenger of Allah." It seems that at that time the Prophet, may Allah bless him and grant him peace, did not have with him anything with which he could pay the debts of his companion. So generosity led him to say to him, "Shall I teach you some words? If you say them, Allah will remove your worry from you and settle your debt for you. You should say in the morning and the evening: 'O Allah, I seek refuge with you from worry and sorrow. I seek refuge with You from incapacity and laziness. I seek refuge with You from miserliness and cowardice. I seek refuge with You from being overcome by debt and overpowered by men.'" Abu Umama said, "I kept on making this supplication until Allah removed my worry from me and settled my debts."

That is how Islam treats the problem of debt in a comprehensive manner which frees the Muslims from excessive love of wealth. The wealthy are encouraged to stand by their Muslim brothers in their time of hardship, and love of wealth does not stop them. They are impelled by the desire to please Allah and His Messenger and this achieves social solidarity in its most beautiful form. Likewise debtors play their role and undertake to repay their debts when Allah opens provision to them, out of their belief that integrity is a mark of honour and the fount of belief and the constitution of Islam. When they are unable to do so, all they can do is to seek refuge with Allah for the forbearance of their creditors and what is greater than wealth and than all the treasures of the earth: the pleasure of Allah and relief from grief on the Day of Rising. Debtors entreat Allah to open for them the gates of His bounty and provide them with good and blessed provision which will release their bonds and liberate them from enslavement to their debts.

O Allah, we praise You and thank You for the bounty which You have bestowed and granted and for making our lives easy for us and illuminating for us the paths of right direction and guidance. Help us to remember You and thank You and worship You well. You are our Master who has brought us out from the darkness to the light. An excellent Master and an excellent Helper!

The obligation of *zakat* and *sadaqa* as the basis of the circulation of wealth in Muslim society

Zakat is the most admirable prescription for the treatment of all the appetites: not only love of wealth, but also love of food, love of hoarding, love of women and children, and all the other appetites which stem from those basic ones. *Zakat* is in fact the means to purify the lower self of a believer from directing all his attention to the desires of the life of this world. It teaches him that others are more entitled to his wealth than he is, once he has satisfied his basic needs. He hears the words of the noble Messenger,

"Anyone who spends the night satisfied while his neighbour is hungry is not one of us." He, may Allah bless him and grant him peace, also said, "When the people of any place spend the night with someone hungry among them, they are no longer entitled to the protection of Allah."

Any Muslim who believes in Allah and pays *zakat* to his brother in Islam will be aware of his need and want to provide for it. If a believer pays out money, which is one the dearest things in life to him and one of his most obdurate appetites, it means that he knows how to overcome his appetites and subject them to his intellect. He rises by this on a celestial spiritual ascent which takes him to the high degree referred to in the *ayat*, *"they prefer them to themselves even if they are in difficulty."* (59:9)

Zakat is an Islamic obligation which achieves a high level of justice and mercy. It does not impose difficulty on the Muslims but rather stimulates the capacity to give and protects them from miserliness and enmity. When the Almighty Master calls for *zakat*, He makes it clear to us that it will purify us and cleanse our spirits and increase our property:

"Take sadaqa *from their wealth to purify and cleanse them and pray for them. Your prayers bring relief to them. Allah is Hearing, Knowing."* (9:103)

Allah praises those who pay *zakat* because they have fulfilled their contract with Allah and consequently merit the vast mercy of Allah:

"He said, 'As for My punishment, I strike with it anyone I will. And My mercy extends to all things. I will prescribe it for those who are godfearing and pay the zakat, and those who believe in Our Signs.'" (7:156)

The Prophet, may Allah bless him and grant him peace, follows the noble Path of the Qur'an in clarifying the importance of *zakat* and its effect on the purification of people's lower selves and the cleansing of their spirits. The Prophet, blessings be upon him, said, "Protect your wealth with *zakat*." He, may Allah bless him and grant him peace, said, "Pay the *zakat* on your property. It is a type of purification which will leave you purified." He said, "When you pay the *zakat* on your property, any evil it contains leaves you." By paying *zakat*, the believer is saved not only from the sin of shirking one of the obligatory duties of the *deen* but also from the bane of the temptation of wealth and greed for it and, in addition, from the rancour of the deprived and the envy of enviers.

The noble Messenger tied the obligation of *zakat* to conscience more than to law. He wanted the believer to free himself from the worship of wealth and for him to use it in ways that are pleasing to Allah and beneficial to His servants. For this reason, the Messenger, may Allah bless him and grant him peace, wanted us to give the *zakat* on our property with a feeling of contentment and happiness, not displeasure and vexation. The Prophet said in the course of one *hadith*, "Give *zakat* and be cheerful about it."

He, may Allah bless him and grant him peace, did not impose *zakat* on money alone, but also on other types of wealth like crops, fruit, and livestock. Because he wanted *zakat* to be a gift of the spirit and the conscience and not an imposition of authority and law, he called on the believers not to stop at giving simply the obligatory amount demanded by *zakat*, but to go beyond that by giving more in the form of *sadaqa*. One day the Prophet was asked about things on which *zakat* did not have to be paid and he replied, "Only this single comprehensive *ayat* has been revealed about them: *'And anyone who did one atom's weight of good will see it. And anyone who did one atom's weight of evil will see it'*" (99:7-8). Everything which a Muslim expends on behalf of his brother is a good which will shine in his balance with Allah.

Anas ibn Malik, may Allah be pleased with him, said, "A man of Tamim came to the Messenger of Allah, may Allah bless him and grant him peace, and said, 'Messenger of Allah. I have a lot of wealth, so tell me how I should act and how I should spend it.' The Messenger said, "Pay the *zakat* on your property. It is a purification which will purify you. Maintain ties with your relatives and acknowledge the rights of the destitute, neighbour, and beggar."

There are many justified demands on people's wealth and justice, social cohesion between Muslims and sharing between them in good and bad times require that revenue should be fairly distributed. When *zakat* was made obligatory for the Muslims it was in order to guarantee the basic needs of the poor and needy. It also served as a training for people's lower selves which are naturally prone to avarice, preventing people from developing excessive love of wealth and promoting love of giving among the individuals of Muslim society.

Zakat in Islam is a sacrifice by means of which the slave thanks his Lord for the blessings He has given him. Because of this, the Messenger, may Allah bless him and grant him peace, called on us to give it with contentment and joyful hearts. He said "You should give the *zakat* on your property cheerfully, paying it every year. You should not give old animals or mangy animals or sick ones but the average of those you possess. Allah does not ask you for the best you have but He does not want the worst."

Zakat is an obligation which should be demanded by those in authority if their consciences do not guide those who refuse to pay it. "Allah will curb by means of the ruler those who are not curbed by the Qur'an." Our Beloved Prophet, may Allah bless him and grant him peace, says, "Anyone who pays the *zakat* owed on his property, hoping for a reward from Allah, will have the reward for it. If anyone refuses to pay it, I will take it, and half of his property on top of it, as one of the dues of your Lord."

Any selfish person who refuses to pay the *zakat* on his property and who, being overcome by love of money, absconds with the rights of Allah over this property, is not left in his error. Instead, *zakat* is taken from him and an additional amount is taken from him as well as a deterrent and punishment for him. We see that the successor of the Messenger of Allah, may Allah bless him and grant him peace, Abu Bakr as-Siddiq, proclaimed in the face of the sedition in which some people became involved when they decided to stop paying the *zakat*: "By Allah, I will fight anyone who makes a distinction between the prayer and *zakat*! *Zakat* is due on wealth. By Allah, if they refuse me a she-goat or hobbling cord which they used to pay to the Messenger of Allah, I will fight them for refusing it!"

Zakat demonstrates the splendid humanity of Islam, seeing it as the right of the poor over the property of the rich. After that no other charge is imposed on the rich, nor are they burdened with any other such duty that is obligatory.

Ibn 'Abbas, may Allah be pleased with him, said, "The Messenger of Allah, may Allah bless him and grant him peace, sent Mu'adh to the Yemen and said to him, 'You are going to a people who have a Scripture, so let the first thing you call them to be the worship of Allah Almighty. If they acknowledge Allah Almighty, then inform them that Allah has made it obligatory for *zakat* to be taken from the wealthy among them and given to their poor. If they obey you in respect of that, beware of taking the things people value highly.'"

This is the advice of the Prophet of mercy who knew the avarice and love of wealth intrinsic to human beings and so he followed a path of mercy in collecting *zakat*, saying, "Beware of taking the things people value highly."

However, what about when people's consciences are dead and their hearts are hardened and, not being able to withstand their love of wealth, they fall into the grip of avarice? The Messenger, may Allah bless him and grant him peace, informed such people that retaliation would follow and that punishment from Allah in store for them. The Prophet, peace and blessings be upon him, said, "There is no one who has gold or silver and does not pay what is due on it without it being turned, on the Day of Rising, into slabs of Fire and being heated in the Fire of Hell and his side, forehead and back being branded with them. Every time they cool down they will be heated up again."

When refusing to pay *zakat* is transformed from being an act of individual disobedience into social disobedience, in other words when a dominant feature of society becomes neglect of *zakat* and refusal to pay it, the sources of provision of that society dwindle and it will be encompassed by disasters of all kinds. The Prophet, may Allah bless him and grant him peace, said, "They do not refuse to pay the *zakat* on their property without being denied rain from heaven."

In this context, being denied rain does not mean only the lack of rain itself, but also the drying up of the sources of wealth and the means of sustenance.

Truly *zakat* is a means of increasing wealth and preserving it with Allah and with people. It is preserved with Allah, because payment of *zakat* is thanking Allah for His blessings and Allah Almighty accepts thankfulness for blessings by giving more of them. And it is preserved with people because when *zakat* is spent in proper and pious ways, it joins ties of kinship, relieves hardship, and helps those in trouble. It also leaves people with warm affection towards the people who have paid *zakat* on their wealth. If wealth is withheld through miserliness, then that affection is replaced by rancour and in place of contentment and supplication there is begrudgement and hatred.

O Allah, we testify to the greatness of Your Message and the trustworthiness of Your Messenger in conveying it. We testify that the Message of Muhammad contains healing for every illness and the required treatment for all the diseases and ailments which afflict human souls.

O Allah, let us be among those who listen to the Word and follow the best of it! Guide us by Your bounty to Your Straight Path and Upright Way! You say - and Your words are true: *"Whoever sees clearly, it is to his own benefit. Whoever is blind, it is to his own detriment."* (6:109) *"Your Lord does not wrong the slaves."* (3:182)

✻✵✻✵✻

So we have browsed in the verdant meadows of both the Qur'an and the *Sunna* in order to see how the All-Wise and All-Aware uses His wise *Shari'a* to treat those appetites which are active in people's lower selves and move them to commit forbidden actions and consequently cause woes for all humanity. We can truly say that our beloved Prophet indeed is the Prophet of Mercy whom Allah sent to protect us from the evils of our lower selves and our evil actions. The *Shari'a* of Allah is a protecting bulwark and defensive shield to restrain the appetites from being let loose to cause ruin and destruction.

However, Allah created both the disease and the remedy to treat it. He appointed the appetites themselves to be an impetus for the establishment of life on the earth and the means of enduring its labours and its pains. This is where the greatness and splendour of Islam lie. He does not charge any self except with as much as it can bear and does not make it bear what it has no power to bear. He makes use of the promptings of the lower self to populate the earth and make life flourish, but at the same time He surrounds those promptings with the unassailable stockade of the *Shari'a* of Allah so that we do not deviate from the path of what is correct, become bewildered in the paths of desires, and end up in the pits of the depths of Hellfire.

Islam takes hold of the hand of the Muslim to guide him with compassion and perseverance to the ladder of the spirit where he is given a drink from the Wine of Purity which enables him to dispense with the impurities of material existence. He comes to know that there is something higher, more sublime and richer than the treasures of this world and what it contains. Once a believer has tasted that, it is easy for him to forgo the world and discipline himself, and his breast is expanded by the Light of Allah.

Islam is the *deen* of both spirit and body, the *deen* of this world and the Next, the *deen* which awakens people's hearts by means of the Qur'an. Then it leaves those with dead consciences to the tender mercies of the ruler who will frighten them with his whip and discipline those who oppose the Straight Path.

However much we were to say or write, our pens would never be able to do justice to the greatness of Islam in respect of its treatment of the sicknesses of man in the most fitting way to provide a sound foundation for human society. We cannot do justice to the incomparable way it heals those societies which follow its guidance and are built on consciences which have been awakened and hearts which have been illuminated by the light of belief.

O Allah! Place us among Your sincere slaves who listen to the Word and follow the best of it! You have said - and Your words are true: *"Those who strive to the utmost in Our way, We will guide them on Our paths."* (29:69)

Chapter Five
The manner with which the righteous men of the past dealt with their appetites

What follows are some examples of the attitudes and statements of our righteous forebears showing us how to strive against the appetites. We mention them as an admonition and lesson for all those with intelligence.

Abu'l-Khayr al-'Asqallani, may Allah be pleased with him, had hankered after fish for years and one day his wish was granted in an entirely lawful way. When he reached out to eat the fish, a sharp bone pierced his finger. He removed his hand, exclaiming, "O Lord, if this is what happens to someone who reaches, out of appetite, for something lawful, what about someone who reaches for something unlawful?"

Abu Sulayman, may Allah be pleased with him, said, "Abandoning one of the appetites of the lower self is more beneficial for the heart than fasting and praying for a year."

In one of the traditions attributed to Allah Almighty we find: "The least I do to a scholar when he prefers his appetite to My love is to deny him the pleasure of intimate conversation with Me."

Abu'l-Hasan ash-Shadhili, may Allah be pleased with him, said, "The *wali* will not reach Allah by any of his appetites or by his own management or any choice of his own."

One of the poets said to explain that the appetites are a kind of bondage into which man falls and shackles which fetter him and disgrace him:

When a blameless lord is captured by his appetites,
he is stripped of his blamelessness and disgraced.
One with appetites is a slave. When he masters appetite,
he becomes a king.

Here are some sayings on the subject which have been passed down to us:

- "Many an appetite bequeaths long-lasting grief."

- "If the heart is nourished by love, the appetites depart."

- "The part the lower self plays in acts of disobedience is clear and evident. The part it plays in acts of obedience is hidden and obscure. It is difficult to treat something which is hidden."

One of the supplications of Ibn 'Ata' Allah al-Iskandari, may Allah be pleased with him, was: "My God! The decree and destiny have overtaken me and desire has taken me captive by the shackles of my appetites. Be my helper and help me and help others by me. Enrich me by Your bounty so that I have no need to seek elsewhere."

Imam Abu'l-Qasim al-Qushayri, may Allah be pleased with him, said, "Having a heart free of distractions is an incomparable blessing. If someone is ungrateful for this blessing, he opens the door of his lower desires by his own hand and is dragged along in the chains of appetite. Allah disturbs his peace of mind and strips away from him the feeling of purity in his heart."

Sayyiduna 'Umar, may Allah be pleased with him, said, "If you fear Allah, you avoid what Allah has forbidden." That means directing yourself sincerely towards Allah, glory be to Him and may He be exalted, dismissing bodily preoccupations, being scrupulous, and sloughing off the chains of the visible world. All this is obtained as a result of fear of Allah, as Allah promises when He says: *"Fear Allah and Allah will teach you."* (2:282)

Lisanu'd-din ibn al-Khatib said, "Know that when any wise artisan reflects on his business and looks at the results, he knows that one day the shop which is his workplace will fall into ruin, his tools wear out, his strength diminish, and the days of his youth disappear. Someone who seizes the time and works hard before his shop falls into disrepair will not need another shop or new tools. He will receive payment for the things he made and can reap the benefit of his labours and enjoy what he has earned. This is a valid metaphor for the soul after the ruin of the body. Hurry then and work hard, hasten and take provision before your shop is ruined and your house destroyed. The best provision is fear of Allah."

If you miss this opportunity that is it. The only time you have is now. There is no other. Anyone who puts things off until tomorrow will never be successful. Man is the child of the moment and so you should be careful not to waste it. Procrastination is the death of action and the enemy of completion. He who embarks rarely fails to arrive. Fortune favours the bold. If anyone puts his faith in time, his hands will tied by the bonds of deprivation. Profit is to be found in boldness. He who lets things slip by is likely to is lose.

Ibn 'Ata', may Allah be pleased with him, said, "Since you know that Shaytan does not ignore you, don't you ignore the One who has your forelock in His Hand." The enemy sees you and you do not see him because of his intense preparations.

I complain of a cunning enemy who has me in his sights
    but I do not see him when he sees me.
If I forget him, he does not forget me.
    O My Master! If you do not help, he will capture me!

Although he sees you and you do not see him, Allah sees him and he does not see Allah. Therefore seek Allah's help against him.

I am afflicted by four enemies attacking me
    with arrows from a bow stretched taut:
Iblis, this world, my self, and low desire.
    My Lord, You have the power to deliver me!

Sufyan ath-Thawri, may Allah be pleased with him, defined the meaning of real asceticism by saying, "It is for a man to be detached in respect of this world when he has wealth and not to desire it when he is poor."

One of the things that Ruwaym al-Baghdadi, may Allah be pleased with him, said is: "Fortitude is to abandon complaint, and contentment is to enjoy affliction, and reliance is to discard secondary means."

Sari as-Saqati, may Allah be pleased with him, said, "Time consists of only three days: yesterday, whose distress, hardship, and sorrow is gone and nothing of it remains; today, in which you are living and which will soon leave you; and tomorrow, of which you have expectations but which you may never see."

It is related from Ibn Siraj that al-Junayd, may Allah be pleased with him, said, "I dreamt of Iblis and he was naked. I asked, 'Are you not ashamed to appear before people like that?' He said, 'By Allah, are those people who are with you? If they were really people, I could have played with them as children play with a ball. They are not people.' I asked him, 'Who are they then?' He said, 'They are in the Shuniziyya Mosque. They have undermined me and weakened me. Whenever I aimed for them, they turned to Allah and I was nearly burned up.' When I woke up I went straight to the Shuniziyya Mosque and there were three men sitting with their heads in their hoods. When they became aware of me, one of them uncovered his head and exclaimed, 'Abu'l-Qasim! Do you believe everything you are told?' They were Abu Hamza, Abu'l-Hasan an-Nuri and Abu Bakr ar-Raqqaq."

One day, the gnostic of Allah, Ibrahim ibn Adham, one of the shaykhs of the ascetics, wanted to eat figs. Not having enough money to buy any, he said to the seller, "Give them to me and I will pay you later." The seller said, "I only sell for cash." So Ibrahim ibn Adham left, saying, "By Allah, I will not eat any figs until the Day of Rising." The seller did not know that it was Ibrahim ibn Adham and when he was told he sent his boy after him who said, "My master has sent these figs to you." Ibrahim ibn Adham said to him, "By Allah, I will not take the figs on any terms." The boy said, "Master, accept this gift. If you do my master will set me free." The shaykh said to him, "That would buy your freedom in this world, but it would mean my enslavement on the Day of Rising."

Abu Bakr ash-Shibli said, "*Jihad* against your own self is better than *jihad* against other people's selves." He used to say, "Someone who is at home with *dhikr* (remembrance) is not the same as someone who is at home with the One who is remembered." He said, "When you find your heart in accord with Allah, beware of your self. When you find your heart in accord with your self, beware of Allah."

O Allah, make us among the people who strive against their lower selves. Give us success in what You love and what pleases You, and join us to the Prophets, the true and martyrs: they are the best companions.

Conclusion
Jihad against the Lower Self

In conclusion I offer my brothers in Islam on the path of belief, a few comments on the vital importance of the struggle against the lower self.

> *"When the whole matter is settled Shaytan will say, 'Allah made you a promise, a promise of truth. I made you a promise and then broke my promise to you. I had no authority over you except that I called you and you responded to me. So do not blame me, but blame yourselves. I cannot come to your aid nor you to mine. I reject the way you made me co-partner with Allah before.' The wrongdoers will have a painful punishment."* (14:22)

Truly the perfect words of Allah are appropriate to every time and place. This *ayat* is applicable to every human experience in which man tastes the bitterness of his disobedience to the Creator and tries to shift responsibility to others in an attempt to absolve his own sly deceitful soul. The Qur'an is explicit in refuting the feeble excuses of every heedless soul and makes the human predicament very clear:

> *"Every self is held in pledge against whatever it has earned."* (74:38)
>
> *"Be fearful of a Day when no self will be able to requite another in any way, nor will any ransom be accepted from it, nor will intercession benefit it, nor will they be helped."* (2:123)

"Every self will be repaid in full for what it did. He best knows the things that they are doing." (39:70)

"On the Day that each self finds the good it did and the evil it did present in front of it, it will wish there were a great distance between it and those things. Allah advises you to beware of Him. Allah is All-Gentle with His slaves." (3:30)

"Remind by it lest a self be delivered up to destruction for what it has earned, not having, apart from Allah, either protector or intercessor. Were it to offer every kind of ransom, that still would not be accepted from it. It is they who are delivered up to destruction for what they have earned. They will have a drink of scalding water and a painful punishment for the way they used to reject." (6:70)

"There and then every self will be tried for what it sent in advance and will be returned to Allah, their Master, the Truth. And what they fabricated will forsake them." (10:30)

"If every self that did wrong possessed everything on earth, it would offer it as a ransom. They shall show their remorse when they see the punishment. Matters will be settled between them with justice. They will not be wronged." (10:54)

"Lest any self should say, 'Alas for my neglect of what was due to Allah, and for being someone who poured ridicule.'" (39:56)

"The Day no soul will possess the power to help another soul in any way. The command that Day will be Allah's." (82:19)

"We do not charge any self beyond what it can bear. With Us is a Book which speaks with Truth. And they will not be wronged." (23:63)

"Anything good that happens to you comes from Allah. Anything bad that happens to you comes from yourself." (4:79)

141

"So fight in the Way of Allah. You bear responsibility for yourself alone." (4:84)

"Read your book! Today your own self is reckoner enough against you!" (17:14)

"Anyone who does evil or wrongs himself and then asks Allah's forgiveness will find Allah All-Forgiving, Most Merciful." (4:110)

"Anyone who commits a wrong action commits it against himself alone. Allah is All-Knowing, All-Wise." (4:111)

"Clear insights have come to you from your Lord. Whoever sees clearly, it is to his own benefit. Whoever is blind, it is to his own detriment." (6:104)

"Anyone who is guided is guided for himself alone. Anyone led astray is led astray only to his own detriment." (17:15)

"Anyone who strives hard against the enemy is striving entirely on his own behalf. Allah is Rich beyond need of any being." (29:6)

"Whoever is purified, is purified for himself alone. To Allah is the journey's end." (35:18)

"In fact, man will be a clear witness against himself in spite of any excuses he might offer." (75:15)

This is a selection of some of the clear *ayats* of Allah which clarify the role of the self in acquiring both good and evil actions in the various stages of its development: the self which commands to evil, the self-reproachful self, and then the self at peace. This last condition is the apex of the stages of the human soul when it returns to its Lord pleased and well-pleasing. (89:28)

After these clear proofs and cogent arguments, how is it possible for any self to complain and offer feeble excuses for its fall into the abyss? How can any intelligent man possessing faith and insight shift the responsibility for his errors onto someone else? Since there is such a precise reckoning for actions, where can you hope to flee to escape their result? Where can you go to escape your evil deeds? So how then can you protect yourself against an evil end result and follow the Path of the *Shari'a* to obtain the blessing of this world and the Next? How? How?

The answer to this question is easy but applying it to your life is not. You are continually surrounded by fearsome waves of materialism raging against you on every side and you have to attempt to rouse your spirit and move your paralysed body to save it from the tempestuous waves and to bring it safely to the solid shore of faith. There is no doubt that this struggle confronts every man. He has to struggle against this world, Iblis, his lower self and appetites. Arrows are fired at him in endless succession. As soon as he saves himself from one arrow another follows it: darkness on top of darkness.

It is a struggle which makes even those with firm resolve among mankind say with a heartfelt cry which echoes through the ages: "If only I had died before this or been something forgotten!" "If only I were dust!" "Alas for what I neglected in respect of Allah!" If it were not for some calming words from the Merciful and Compassionate, the hearts of the believers would have burst out of regret for the mistakes they made during their struggle to gain dominance over their appetites, in spite of their heroic attempts to prevent decline and their even more difficult struggle for spiritual development. Those luminous words are:

> *"Say: O My slaves who have been profligate against yourselves, do not despair of the mercy of Allah. Allah forgives all wrong actions."* (39:53)

Anyone who studies the *ayats* of forgiveness and mercy and the *hadiths* of the Prophet about that will discover that they are very numerous and the ignorant are deluded by that abundance into having almost too good an opinion of Allah. This demonstrates profound ignorance of the fundamentals of Islamic belief. Those *ayats* and *hadiths* which deal with forgiveness are primarily there as waymarks on the path of those who strive in the Way of Allah. As for the path of the heedless - We seek refuge with Allah! - for them they are red signs warning of danger and an evil outcome.

Hence there is a strong warning given to those who leave this world with no provision, saying, "We had a good opinion of Allah." That is a terrible lie against themselves and great self-deception. If they had truly had a good opinion of Allah, they would have performed good actions as the Protected Truthful Messenger said.

O my God! How is it possible for us to do good actions when remarkable men, so much greater than us, have complained to You of how long the path is and how little provision they have?

O my God! How can we face all those struggles alone if You are not beside us?

O my God! *"Our Lord, we heard a caller calling to belief: 'Believe in your Lord!' and we believed. Our Lord, forgive us our wrong actions and erase our bad actions from us and let us die with the people of true piety."* (3:193)

O my God! We have believed in You and Your beloved chosen Messenger, so be our help against the temptations we encounter in our lives in this world and the prompting of the self and the appetites and Shaytan.

We listen to Your blessed words, *" If an evil prod from Shaytan goads you on, seek refuge in Allah. He is All-Hearing, All-Seeing."* (7:200) And then we hear, *"Those who are godfearing, when they are bothered by a visitation from Shaytan, remember, and immediately see clearly."* (7:201)

We must implement these directives, but we also call on You, O Allah, to relieve the believers of the harassment of satanic proddings and their ills, and to guide them in their spiritual ascent. The heart should be humble and the eye should weep. The self should burst with regret for what it has neglected in respect of Allah.

O Allah! Be gentle to us and save us from the wastelands and perils of our selves. You have power over everything and are the Answerer of our prayers.

O Allah! Do not take us to task for our sins and bad actions, but treat us as befits Your generosity and magnanimity. Make our slips few and forgive our mistakes, veil our errors, and spare us the evils of our selves and our bad actions. How can we be saved if You do not help us? Indeed how can we have faith if You do not surround us with Your generous pardon and great gentleness? The oceans of Your generosity are boundless and Your sincere slaves travel upon them acknowledging Your gifts and boundless generosity.

Brothers in belief! The struggle which we face in our lives is the touchstone of the trials which Allah created us for, a task which the heavens and earth were unable to bear! *"They refused to take it on and were very wary of it. And man took it on. He is indeed wrongdoing and ignorant"* (33:72). So we must strive against our lower self which commands to evil. It has the promise of the Garden and yet it leads us to the Fire. It loves the ornaments and adornments of this world and dislikes the places and hardships of good. It is not possible to be saved from its snares and rescued from its ruses except by clinging to the firm rope of Allah and His luminous path and travelling on the path of the noble Qur'an and the *Sunna* of the Beloved Prophet. Millions have travelled this path spending their lives in the greater *jihad,* which is the *jihad* against the lower self, until they met their Lord with their self at peace, pleasing and well-pleased, free of the bondage of the lower self and the abasement of enslavement to other than Allah - and what an despicable abasement that is!

O Allah! Bless and grant peace to our Master Muhammad, the medicine and cure of hearts and the healing and well-being of bodies, who was sent as a mercy to all beings to free them from the evil of their selves and their bad actions.